Crazy Women Killers

Tanya Bermudez

Published by Trellis Publishing, 2021.

CRAZY WOMEN KILLERS

First edition. July 4, 2021.

Copyright © 2021 Tanya Bermudez.

ISBN: 979-8224038916

Written by Tanya Bermudez.

CRAZY WOMEN KILLERS
TANYA BERMUDEZ

Michelle Gable wanted out.

Growing up in Maryland, she hated the big city. So when she married Joe she insisted that they lived someplace as clean as pure as they could find.

They chose Helena, Montana.

An Air Force serviceman, Joe and Michelle had married at Andrews Air Force Base in Maryland in 1986. The two would move to Washington state and North Dakota before settling in Montana in 2003.

But the clean air and beautiful snow peaks were not enough to satisfy Michelle.

She spent her days cleaning and scrubbing the floor. When she grew tired of that, she moved to scrubbing the windows. Then the kitchen. Then the back porch.

Anything to clean her home of the "chemicals" that radiated from the town.

"It stinks in here!" Michelle said when her husband strolled his way into the kitchen for breakfast.

Joe sniffed the air. "I don't smell anything."

"You're not in tune like me," Michelle screamed. "Can't you smell that? That's pollution. That's poison. Its going to kill us."

Joe could only watch as his wife ransacked a closet full of bicarbonate soda. She poured the contents into a bucket of water and began to scrub down the kitchen counter.

Joe would leave for work. When he would return home, his wife would not greet him with open arms.

"Hey babe," Joe said, reaching for his wife.

"You stink!" Michelle said. "You smell like gasoline. Or pesticides! Go take a shower!"

Michelle's erratic behavior would register with the local police department. On September 27, 2003, Michelle would call police to file a missing person report on her husband. She stated that he left on his

Harley Davidson motorcycle on the 26th and had not been heard from since. Joe, however, would return two days later.

On June 20th 2004, Michelle called the police again to inform them that Joe had pushed her off his Harley Davidson. She was taken to the emergency room where she complained of shortness of breath with a headache. The staff could not find any signs of injury.

In a court video, Michelle would describe that she loved Joe despite his alleged abuse.

"It wasn't the first time (when he pushed he from a motorcycle)," Michelle said. "I love this man more than anything no matter what he will do to me in life. He was troubled. He sniffed glue and gas when he was a kid. Then he was sent to a Christian reform school before he joined the Air Force."

Michelle would not limit her irrational wrath to just her husband. Her neighbors and their gardeners also got a taste of her nuttiness.

"What the hell are you doing?" Michelle screamed from her window at the Mexican gardener mowing both hers and the neighbor's lawn.

Startled, the old landscaper turned the engine on the lawnmower off.

Michelle came stomping out of her door.

"What the hell are you doing?"

"I'm sorry?"

"I can't breathe," Michelle pointed at the lawnmower. "What are you doing? You're contaminating the air. That shit is going everywhere. Pesticides!"

Her neighbor then came to ask what the commotion was about. Michelle didn't hold back.

"You people have no idea what you're doing. No idea!"

Michelle began to cough uncontrollably, covering her mouth. She turned her back to the duo and ran back into her house.

"What was that all about?" the neighbor asked.

"She crazy," the gardener said. "Loco en la cabeza."

It would turn out that her own lawn was being mowed at the request of her own landlord.

"Upon my arrival," the investigating police officer said. "The lawn was being mowed and she was in the street screaming at them to stop. She stated she was having trouble breathing and asked for an ambulance. But when the ambulance arrived, she refused transport or further medical attention. The property manager also came to the Cutler Street home (Michelle's residence), telling officers he was on vacation and hadn't been able to return her phone calls from her asking him to delay having the lawn mowed.Michelle was very angry and feels like she's been ignored. She stated her life was in danger today and wants to make sure it doesn't happen again. While I was present, (the property manager) and Michelle came to an agreement that she or her husband will mow the lawn from now on. She was claiming that the lawn mowers the other people were using had pesticides on them which made her sick."

Michelle spent her days sleeping and cleaning, cleaning and sleeping. Her husband Joe chalked it up to Michelle just being 'Michelle'. Michelle's phobia regressed to the point where she didn't even want to leave the house.

But in 2009, personal tragedy would make its way into Michelle's life. Her mother, to whom she was very close, would pass away.

Michelle became distraught. She and Joe trekked to Maryland for the funeral but only Joe made it home. Michelle wanted to stay behind to tie up some 'loose ends.' But she would end up remaining in her hometown for over a year. Joe would call and ask what was going on but the phone calls became less and less frequent.

Joe decided to move on and began seeing a female friend.

Her name was Sunday Bennett. She was pushing fifty years old but she had a youthful exuberance that had long disappeared from Michelle's persona. They met through a Facebook game called

"Vampire Wars." The two would hang out, taking in a movie then chomp on cheese and sip wine. Sunday was married like Joe but estranged from her spouse like Joe was himself.

For the first time in a long while, Joe felt happy.

Thoughts of Michelle faded from his mind until a morning in September of 2011.

A day when Michelle finally came home.

She arrived at the house early and crept up the steps. In the guest bedroom, she saw Sunday sleeping on an air mattress.

Enraged she stomped into her own bedroom and punched a sleeping Joe in the arm.

"Wake up!"

"Wha-"

"Wake up, asshole."

"The hell is going on?"

"That's what I'm asking you," Michelle hissed. "Who the hell is that woman?"

"Her name is Sunday."

"What the fuck is a Sunday doing in my house?"

"Its a long story," Joe stammered. "We stayed up a bit too late. Talking."

"Talking?"

"She's just a friend, okay?" Joe put up his hands to placate his wild-eyed wife. "A friend."

Joe woke up his lady friend. He explained about his wife, stating that this was all unexpected. The calm Sunday just nodded her head and went about her daily routine of making coffee for her and Joe.

Only this time, Michelle was waiting for her on the couch.

"Do you like sugar in your coffee?" Sunday asked.

"No," Michelle snapped.

Sunday poured out a cup for Michelle as all three of them sat in the nook of the kitchen.

After a minute of tense silence, Michelle stood up.

"Let's go have breakfast!"

Sunday didn't reply immediately. She gave a sideways glance to Joe. Joe said nothing.

"I don't think that's a good idea," Sunday finally said with a smile.

"Don't think it's a good idea?" Michelle screamed.

"No."

"Am I not good enough for you? You think you're better than me, goddammit!"

"That's enough," Joe stood up, standing between Michelle and the still seated Sunday.

"Get up, bitch! Get up and get the hell out of my house!"

"No," Joe said. "You leave."

"What?"

"You need to leave!"

Joe pushed back against his wife, leading her out the door.

Humiliated, Michelle didn't fight back. She checked into a motel and plotted her revenge.

Meanwhile, Joe tried to patch things up with Sunday. His friend had been rattled but she understood.

Joe was married to a nut job.

Michelle would return the following day while Joe changed the locks. She demanded to be let in the home so that she could get her clothes.

Sifting through her drawers, the nose that had once been so sensitive to chemicals now became ultra-sensitive to the smell of another female in the home. She firmly believed that Sunday had taken Michelle's place when she was gone for over two years.

Michelle then began stalking the couple.

She waited for them outside her car, taking her pictures. She photographed her coming to and from work. She photographed the couple hugging.

Michelle had been completely dependent on Joe for her finances. Now with this other woman in the picture, her money flow was at risk.

Michelle would never be able to hold down a job.

She couldn't with her growing mental disorder. But if she really put her mind to it, Michelle Gable could have made a great private investigator.

The information she gathered on Sunday could not have been accomplished better by a professional. She found out where Sunday worked, found out about her estranged husband and basically everything she could about her competitor's life.

Joe commanded her to stop. He told her the marriage had been over when she decided not to return after her mother's funeral.

The next day, Joseph Gable filed a petition for a temporary order of protection in Lewis and Clark District Court. He said his wife lived in Maryland and they were married but separated. He said his wife was intimidating him, had held him against his will and was stalking him.

The restraining order stated that as Joseph Gable was changing the locks on the house between 9:30 and 10 a.m. on Sept. 20, his wife came inside and she said "I'm here to get my shit."

Once inside, Michelle threw his laptop computer down the stairwell which broke it into pieces. She then stormed out of the house and parked her car behind his in the driveway to block his exit.

"She has been out of Montana on the East Coast in Maryland for over two years, came back unannounced and is now trying to disrupt my life any way she can apparently," Joe wrote in the restraining order request.

But the judge refused.

The judge saw no immediate threat to the well being of Joe or his girlfriend Sunday.

Joe decided not to stop with just the restraining order. He filed for divorce from Michelle.

When Michelle received the papers, she went berserk. She called a friend from a motel who then called police to do a welfare check on her. Ignoring suggestions to get mental hep, she decided to take her stalking to a whole other level.

Parking outside her former home, Michelle waited until all the lights were out and the couple were asleep.

She then quietly broke in through the back door and paced throughout the home. Her plan was to surprise Joe in the morning and try to win him back.

Michelle rummaged through drawers while looking for some kind of incriminating evidence to use against Sunday. She came upon Sunday's phone and nearly screamed with glee.

"Jackpot," she whispered.

Scrolling through Sunday's contacts, she found the number of her estranged husband. She then sent him a text stating that "Joe's wife loves him very much but I am sleeping with him…Joe's wife really loves him but i convinced him to get rid of her."

Michelle wrote the message as if she were Sunday in the hopes of getting back at her.

Joe was an early riser and he went downstairs in his tank top and boxer shorts, rubbing sleep rocks out of his eyes.

Not only did he not know that Michelle had broken in but that she had armed herself with a .38 caliber revolver and a .9mm pistol.

"The hell are you doing here?"

"What's she doing here!" Michelle screamed pointing both guns at his chest. The two stared at each other for what seemed like an eternity until Joe struck. He grabbed Michelle by both wrists as she screamed obscenities.

She started firing the weapon, forcing Joe to release his grip.

Backing away, Joe could only hope for mercy from the psychopath.

"I loved you, Joe! I loved you and this is how you betray me? This is how you treat me!"

"Michelle," Joe pleaded. "I need you to calm down."

"I loved you with all my heart! And you traded me for that bitch!" Michelle screamed, shooting Joe in the shoulder then near the heart.

Awakened by the commotion, Sunday sprinted down the steps only to be confronted by Michelle.

"You," Michelle said. "You caused all this."

Sunday had nowhere to run. She sidestepped Michelle and opened a side door which led to the basement.

"You can't hide," Michelle screamed. "I told you all along. You can't hide from me, you bitch!"

"Michelle, please," Sunday said, trying to barricade herself in to no avail. "I'm so sorry."

"You took my husband!"

Michelle pointed the gun at the woman who had tormented her for all these weeks.

She showed Sunday no mercy.

Michelle let loose with both barrels, hitting her adversary six times.

Meanwhile, Joe crawled out to the living room and dials 911.

Officers arrived with guns drawn. They saw the wounded Joe on the ground, bleeding from his nose, mouth and extremities.

"My wife," Joe whispered. "My wife did this."

But as they journeyed through the home, they would find Michelle laying on her side and holding her stomach.

"Sunday did it," Michelle said. "She shot me. She shot Joe. She's in the basement."

The police now did not know who to believe. They think that they have a live shooter holed up in the basement.

Once backup arrived, they moved down to confront the shooter.

It had been over an hour of waiting for the wounded Sunday. By the time police entered the basement, she had succumbed from her wounds.

Joe would die as well, bleeding out on the living room floor.

Michelle's wounds were limited to a few scratches, courtesy of Joe.

Once in the interrogation room, the detectives scrutinized her story and expressed disbelief. Michelle then changed her story again, stating that she shot Joe but that she did it out of self-defense.

"They both came for me," Michelle said. "They both came at me and I had no choice."

Michelle's stupidity would prove to be her undoing.

She had broken into the home with two guns then claimed self-defense.

Michelle would tell police that the Joe came at her with a gun or "maybe two" and that she caught her finger in the gun as she defended herself.

"The gun went off with my finger in it," Michelle said. "Then we struggled and the gun went off."

The crime scene investigation would later reveal that Michelle shot Joe and Sunday a combined seventeen times.

But Michelle claimed that Joe came at her because he was upset about some money that she had withdrawn from their account.

"Sunday only wanted him for his money," Michelle pleaded. "I was only trying to protect him. So I took out $10,000 without telling anyone."

Michelle would be found guilty on two counts of first degree murder. She would receive one-hundred years for each murder but continues to appeal.

SHE DEVIL: THE TRUE STORY OF MYRA HINDLEY

ELLEN THOMAS

In the early 1960s, Myra Hindley took her first job out of school at a small chemical company called Millwards Merchandise. A shy eighteen-year-old, she kept to herself, reading in the office courtyard during breaks.

But she only did this to attract her co-worker, Ian Brady.

Brady would spend his breaks reading books. Myra soon followed suit in the hopes that he would approach.

After several months, the Glasgow, Scotland native finally made his move.

They both worked at the office as clerks. Brady was four years older than her as they began to date.

Myra lived with her grandmother and gave her virginity to the awkward co-worker on her grandmother's sofa. She would soon become Brady's accomplice in some of the most gruesome child killings in the history of Great Britain.

A BAD NEWS CHARACTER

Brady already had a police record for petty theft. He also had a strange demeanor, tilting his head oddly at people as he stared them down with hooded eyes.

He was nicknamed "Lassie", not a reference to the Collie dog but to his feminine body language. Brady was tall, skinny and would indicate later that he was a bisexual. As a child, he had few friends and was called "Dracula" in the neighborhood. He would torture kittens and see how long it took for them to die.

They were both bookworms and Brady would give Myra books on the Marquis De Sade, trying to introduce her to the world of sexual sadism. After their dates, he would invite her back to his place and play back recordings of Adolph Hitler's speeches.

The young couple would come up with pet nicknames for each other. Myra would call Ian "Hetty" after a character in the Goons and he would call her "Hess" after Hitler's deputy. They would soon become inseparable, both strangely odd people that felt that were superior and set apart from everyone else.

It soon became clear, however, that Ian was influencing Myra and not the other way around. He was her guide to the world of sexual sadism and then later, slowly revealed his desire to rape and murder children.

He started this by sharing a book in the same way he introduced her to sadomasochism. The book had detailed the "crime of the century". A child was the victim and one of the characters was named Myra.

"He had given me a book called 'Compulsion,'" Myra recalled. "Which was the story of Leopold and Loeb. They decided to commit the perfect murder. They were studying the philosophy of Nietzsche, his theory of the superiority of the pure Aryan and the strong overcoming the weak. It was very much the Nazi philosophy. They kidnapped a twelve-year-old boy for a ransom. They killed him, were caught and sent to prison. I told him it was a very disturbing book. But why exactly had he wanted me to read it? He told me he wanted to do a perfect murder and I was going to help him. That was why he needed me to pick someone up as I was a woman and a child would be more trusting of a woman. I burst into tears and he slapped my head backward and forward. I managed to fight him off and told him to stop it."

Myra fell prey to Ian's system of push and pull psychology. He would be abusive to Myra then inexplicably turn around and be sweet to her.

"I must be totally honest and say he wasn't always cruel and sadistic towards me," Myra said. "We had some pleasant times in country places that he'd found during his travels on his bike. We'd pack a picnic lunch, lots of coffee, bottles of wine and spend whole days in peace and tranquility. That was such a contrast to the other side of him. These were moments I treasured and thought about when things were bad. Trying to remember, telling myself that he couldn't help what he was and maybe in time he would become accustomed to ordinary domesticity and we could live a normal life."

IDLE HANDS

"Myra was a bored English girl looking for some adventure," forensic psychologist Paula Orange said. "Brady had an edge about him. Myra liked that about him, she wanted out of her dull life and into a world of edgy darkness, if you will."

Myra didn't judge Brady for being an avowed Nazi. She thought he was just going through a phase but he continued to play Richard Wagner's music full blast and storm around the house dressed up in Nazi regalia. Working himself up into a frenzy, he would then play rough sex games with Myra.

Myra found this aspect of Brady's personality to be alluring. She enjoyed dressing up in leather and black stockings, indulging whatever fantasy Brady could come up with.

"She was a sheltered young woman," Orange said. "And Brady opened up a whole new world to her. Think of it as 'Fifty Shades of Grey' with some Nazism thrown in and you have the whole relationship of Myra Hindley and Ian Brady."

The kinky sex continued and Brady gave stronger indications that he wanted to commit the perfect murder.

He wanted to harm children.

But he needed an accomplice.

"We can make the case that Myra made the jump from sadomasochistic sex to murder out of an obligation to Ian," Orange said. "It gave her a rush, to follow his lead. She needed more and more to get that same high."

The two would feed off each other sexually after which Ian would begin to plot the murders out. Who would be their victim? How would they kill them? Where would they kill them? He wrote things out in advance to the most minute detail.

"She (Myra) became desperate to fulfill his fantasies, his needs," journalist Clint Entwhistle said. "She was frightened, I suspect, of rejection by him."

So Myra didn't report him. She went along with his program.

SNAPPED

Brady had made his decision that they were going to kill someone. The night before, he took Myra to a bar on the back of his motorcycle. The two parked a little beyond the pub itself. Ian then began to intimidate Myra. He was jealous that she took a ride home from a co-worker.

"All the time we were talking," Myra recalled. "He was running a knife across his fingers. I honestly thought he was going to stab me. Then he laughed, put the knife away, told me never to accept a lift (the co-worker) again, and we drove back to the pub."

"Later as we were driving home, I dreaded what he would do when we got there, for I knew he would do something. "He raped me anally, urinated inside me and, whilst doing so, began strangling me until I nearly passed out. Then he bit me on the cheekbone, just below my right eye, until my face began to bleed. I tried to fight him off strangling me and biting me, but the more I did, the more the pressure increased. Before he left, when he'd seen the state of my face, he told me to stay off work the next day ..."

This would all take place under the roof of Myra's grandmother who was asleep when the assault took place.

"My gran almost fainted when she saw me and went to get my mother, who asked me if 'He' had done that to me. My mother disliked him intensely and kept telling me he was no good for me; she'd been telling me that since I'd met him at 18 and a half, but what girl of that age listens to her mother when she is wholly infatuated and in love? I told them what he had told me to say (she had been hit by a beer bottle during a bar fight) but I knew they didn't believe me."

THE FIRST MURDER

The following night after he beat down Myra, Brady selected his first victim.

He spotted a teenage girl walking to a dance by herself. She wore a sky blue jacket over a button-down red polka dot dress. Her white gloves and high heels turned on Ian Brady but what really arrested his attention was her face.

Cute with an air of innocence. A face that had an easy vulnerability, someone who would crack under the pressure of his whip.

Her pain and tears would be delicious, Ian thought.

Her name was Pauline Reede.

Brady gave Ian her orders and told her to pick the girl up. He would follow them on his bike.

"Ian Brady was awkward," Entwistle said. "He was not the kind of person a child would trust. There is no way anyone would have gotten into a car with him."

That is what he needed Myra for.

Myra did as he said, driving up alongside Pauline as she walked on the deserted road. The two young woman had already known each other from around the neighborhood.

"Can I give you a lift?" Myra asked.

"Oh, thank you, sure," Polly got into the small white van.

"Where are you going?"

"To the dance hall-"

"Okay," Myra said. "I just have to go to the Moors. I just lost one of my gloves. You can help me look for it. It will only take a second."

Pauline simply nodded her head. She trusted Myra.

THE KILLING FIELDS

"The Moors above Manchester were a special place for Ian Brady and Myra Hindley," Entwistle said. "They picnicked there together. They'd have sex there. It was a very, very important place to them."

It would also be the place where they would commit their first murder together.

Myra stepped off the van and directed Polly to look through some bushes. It was dark and Pauline asked if they should just look for it in the morning. Myra laughed it off and walked away, feigning as if she were looking for her gloves.

Ian Brady waited in the bushes, his mouth dry with anticipation, as he watched the sixteen-year-old Polly sift through the bushes.

Sneaking behind his victim, he slammed her across the head with a shovel.

Pauline Reede fell to the ground, stunned.

She would then be raped, tortured then murdered by the sadistic Brady.

"Brady was a sadist," Orange said. "He got off on the suffering of his young victim. The more innocent she was, the more she screamed, the more she pleaded for her life, the more he got off. It was part of the high for him. He had moved beyond the bedroom thrills with Myra and needed a bigger high. He wanted his fantasy to become reality."

Brady assaulted Pauline until she lost consciousness.

No longer able to provide him the "fun" of listening to her suffer, he took a knife to her throat and killed her.

Myra watched in silence as Ian Brady commit the brutal crime and then proceeded to bury Polly in a shallow grave.

"He led me to her body which I tried not to look at," Myra wrote. "I didn't know at the time that he was testing me at there was no need for me to be there. He told me to look at here. I'll never be able to forget what I saw. I stood and looked at the dark outline of the rocks against the horizon of the dark sky. Three people died that night. Pauline. My soul. And God. No God would have let what had happened, happen."

On the surface, however, Myra didn't seem distressed about the murder. She went to work the following Monday as if nothing happened.

"You would think if she had any conscience left she would have gone to the authorities," Orange said. "But Myra had been dehumanized by that point. The daily rapes and assaults made her numb to everything."

Still, a part of her old self remained. The disappearance of Pauline Reade sent shockwaves throughout Manchester. Myra was reading the newspaper one day and noticed a personal column written by Pauline Reade's mother.

It read " Pauline, please come home. We're heartbroken for you."

"I began to cry," Myra recalled. "Rocking myself back and forth with the paper clutched to my chest. I didn't hear his bike, nor knew that he'd come into the house. He asked me what was wrong but I couldn't answer; I couldn't stop shaking and crying, for I was devastated about what had happened to Pauline, and for her mum and dad. I really liked Mrs. Reade and used to feel sorry for her because she had problems with her nerves and always looked as though she was on the edge of a breakdown. He grabbed the paper off me and soon saw what I'd seen."

"He put the bolt on the front door in case gran came back, did the same to the back door, and began to strangle me. Before I lost consciousness, I heard him remind me of what he'd said after Pauline's murder, and that threat still stood. After the first murder, as we were driving home, he told me that if I'd shown any signs of backing out, I would have finished up in the same grave as Pauline."

MYRA'S EARLY LIFE

As one would expect, Myra grew up in an abusive home.

Her parents engaged in daily shouting matches which she watched from behind her bedroom door.

Her father would routinely beat her mother, exposing Myra to sudden violence during her formative years. He was a competitive boxer who would also engage in weekend bar brawls.

"He used to beat her a lot," Entwhistle said. "Her father was a very, very powerful influence on her life. She had a tough personality type to start with. If you combine that with a violent childhood, a childhood where she was taught how to be violent, how to be aggressive, then you end up with an unusual personality type."

Myra hated her father and saw him as a bully. He would teach her to box, often hitting her across the head when she performed the techniques incorrectly.

"My father wielded total parental control," Myra said. "I rebelled against it. Fought against it. All my life until I was old enough to free myself from it. All his attempts to control me, even the successful ones were at great cost and were the result of bitter recriminations and often a hard physical punishment."

Myra's father would give her spankings without warning, leaving her buttocks bruised.

Once when she was bullied by a little boy and came home with bruises on her face, her father locked her out of the house. He told her to either face down the bully or he was going to beat her up himself.

"I set up the street to meet my persecutor," Myra recalled. "I quickly concentrated on whatDad had told me and showed me. As Kenny's hand came up, I shot up my left hand, fist bunched towards his head. As I predicted, both hands went up to protect his face and I lifted my right hand and slammed it into his tummy, hitting him hard. With a gasp, Kenny Holden's knees crumbled and before he could recover I slammed my left fist into the side of his head. Kenny was so heavily shocked he sat down heavily on the floor and burst into tears. I stood looking down at him triumphantly."

Myra saw a lot of her father in Ian Brady. Aggressive. Ultra-violent.

"Myra did what we call in psychology, 'transference,'" Orange said. "She saw in Ian what she saw in her father. She never got her daddy's love. So in her mind, she saw Ian as Daddy. She wanted Daddy's love and would do whatever Ian wanted. That was part of her cycle. Transferring a deep need for her father's love onto Ian. There is the strong possibility that had Myra never hooked up with Ian she would have never become a murderer. But the two of them together? Horrific results."

"The bringing together of Myra Hindley and Ian Brady," Entwhistle said. "Unleashed an appalling set of criminal acts."

POLLY IS STILL MISSING

The disappearance of Polly Reede sent the town of Manchester on edge. Things like that simply didn't happen there.

"The fact that children were being abducted and killed," Entwhistle said. "Was incomprehensible to the ordinary man and woman in the street."

Myra would soon find out that Ian's sexual fantasies were not limited to teenaged girls.

He wanted boys too.

Myra would again be a willing accomplice in procuring Ian's second victim. This time, it would be twelve-year-old John Killbride. Myra would befriend the young boy before bringing him to the Moors where he would be sexually assaulted by Brady and later killed.

"I had a terrible feeling something had happened to him," John Killbridge's mother recalled when her son didn't come home from school. "Because he wasn't the kind of boy who would leave home for any reason. He was quite happy and very pleasant, always singing and whistling and I just couldn't see him going anywhere with anyone. Unless it was in an innocent way, somebody wanting to do a job with him or something like that. He'd be enticed into a car that way."

Ian would take photos of the body and burial site. This would become part of their ritual, their ceremony. They would perform the murder then take photographs as if to mark the moment. Then they would return to the scene of the crime days after with their dog "Puppet" in tow. They would take more pictures and relive what took place only days earlier.

"He stopped me as I was walking (to take a picture)," Myra recalled. "And said to turnaround. Moved me about a bit. Told me to kneel down and look at 'Puppet' whose head was showing when he was still wrapped inside my coat. I now know, and knew quite soon afterward, that he photographed me virtually kneeling on John Killbride's grave."

AN INSATIABLE HUNGER

Four months had elapsed between the Pauline and John Killbride murders. But now Ian could not wait long. He ordered Myra to deliver another victim to the isolated Moors.

His name was Keith Bennett. An exuberant, trusting boy, Keith looked like the proverbial nerd with a gap-toothed smile and professorial eyeglasses.

"Keith was a cheeky little lad," Entwhistle said. "He liked to go out and have fun."

Trusting that Myra was taking him some place fun, the young Keith was ambushed by Brady who wrapped a cord around his neck.

Myra did her usual best to remain detached while the horrific attack took place.

"I hadn't wanted this to happen," Myra recalled. "I was tense and terrified. I tried to concentrate my mind miles away from where I was. Finally, after roughly what I think was a half an hour by which time dusk began to descend. I heard him whistle or call. When I stood up, he was waving me back down to the stream bed. Virtually nothing was said as we made our way back except for him saying the spade was hampering him and he'd have to hide it, which he did."

The twelve-year-old Keith, whose entire family was waiting for him at his grandmother's house, never showed up.

His entire family would be traumatized for life.

"I am a mother," Keith's mother, Winnie Johnson said. "It was my first lad and I've got to find him no matter what."

Keith Bennett's body was never found.

"I have nightmares," Johnson said. "I jump in my sleep. It's getting to me now. Because I just can't get him back."

Meanwhile, Myra and Ian would once again take mementos of their time together, taking photos of themselves along the Moors on Keith's fresh grave. Days later, the two would go to St. James Church for midnight mass.

"I retained a warm religious glow," Myra said. "And came out feeling warmed. Not so Ian who took a long swill of whiskey and went to the grave where he casually urinated."

RITUALS

The photos of their time together became an obsession for Ian Brady. He had an automatic camera where he would set the timer and pose for photographs with Myra. In a few of them, they would pose on top of the fresh graves with Ian playfully choking Myra.

"Myra and Ian would often return to the scenes of their crimes," Orange said. "They would take photos of themselves there and relive the thrill of committing the murders."

Over time, however, the photos would not be enough stimulation. They needed something better. Something more visceral.

Sounds.

Ian Brady decided he would record the audio of their next victim being tortured.

That next victim would be ten-year-old Leslie Ann Downey. Myra would befriend and abduct her from the county fairgrounds.

"They would take her back to their home," Entwistle said. "Where he photographed her and recorded her being tortured."

Ian Brady would listen to the audio tape over and over again, closing his eyes and remembering the horrific acts he committed.

Is is the murder of Leslie that Myra would refuse to talk about in interviews.

"There's a tape that isn't what people think it is," Myra said, trying to downplay her own sadism evident in the tapes. "But it's bad. I just hurt so much to think that I've been such a cruel bastard."

THE RUSH OF KILLING

Like a drug addict needing a bigger hit to get high, Brady needed more and more of a thrill for his next murder. He started to get sloppy whereas before his attacks were meticulously planned out.

His next victim would be Edward Evans.

"Edwards was sixteen, seventeen years old," Entwhistle said. "And he picked him up in a pub in Manchester."

This would be the first time Ian acted in tandem with Myra to obtain the victim. They enticed the young man to come over to their home and there were witnesses in the pub.

The couple also invited Myra's brother in law, Dave Smith to watch the carnage.

"Smith had no idea what was going on," Entwhistle said. "He walked into it totally cold, totally unaware and soon found out that he was involved in the most horrific scene with blood all over the place. A man's head being smashed in."

Smith was appalled, then called the police and told them of the killing.

Police arrived on scene within minutes. They discovered the mauled body of Edwards in a tub. Both Ian and Myra would be arrested.

"It is inexplicable as to why the couple would allow Dave Smith to witness the murder," Orange said. "A part of me thinks that it was part of increasing the thrill. The desire to share what they felt was a special moment with someone else."

A CHILLING DISCOVERY

Investigators would then scour the home, finding one unusual clue that would reveal the goings on of the couple now known in the papers as the Moors Murderers.

They found a left over luggage ticket.

The police would go to the central train station and matched the ticket with a suitcase. Inside, the found something they would never forget.

"They kept trophies in suitcases," Entwhistle said. "In there, of course, was the tape recording of Leslie Ann Downey and that proved what they'd done."

The police would play back the tapes. It churned their stomach to hear the tearful cries of Leslie Ann Downey plead for her life.

"You need to do what he says," Hindley screamed at the little girl. "I told you to shut your face!"

"I want to go home," the little girl pleaded.

"Quiet! Do you not speak English?"

The tape would be played for the jurors at the trial of the couple.

According to witnesses, you could hear a pin drop when they played the tape in court.

"Afterward there was a long, stony silence," Entwhistle said. "As people reflected on what they just heard."

DENIAL

Myra would maintain her own innocence of the murders and repeatedly state that she never witnessed any of the killings herself.

"My solicitor (defense attorney) told me they'd found the body of a child," Myra said. "Identified as Lesley Ann Downey, did I know anything about it? And I said 'No.' A week after that, I'm not sure, they found John Killbride's body and they charged me with, I think it was the murder of John Killbride. Yes, it was.They set me down behind a table and behind it was a large poster of John Killbride. 'Will you just identify these pictures or these photos and tell us if you seen them before.' I'd say, yes, and then they turned over the picture to another photo of the unearthed body of John Killbride."

The picture, Myra would state, made her cry.

LETTERS TO MOMMA

Myra would write her mother numerous letters before her trial. She would order her mother to destroy the letters after she read them but her mother thought otherwise. She would also tell her mother to keep the photographs of her and Ian to herself.

"Don't believe what they're saying about us," Myra wrote. "It is all lies."

But the mothers of all the victims didn't see it that way.

In court, they all had an opportunity to confront Myra.

"The worst part was being confronted by Mrs. West in the witness box," Myra recalled. "And I was looking at her as she was giving evidence and she saw me looking at her and she screamed across at me. 'How can you look at me?' And she called me every name under the sun."

It is at this point that Myra stated that she began to fully realize the gravity of her crimes.

"It suddenly hit me just what I'd done and I think he (Ian) sensed this," Myra said. "We were sitting next to each other and he just put his hand on my arm and squeezed my arm. And I turned around and looked at him, and he was telling me with his eyes to keep quiet."

The jury would find them guilty and in May of 1966 both would be sentenced to life in prison.

STANDING BY HER MAN

Myra refused to testify against Ian. There were some legal experts at the time who believed that if she gave evidence against Brady she would have walked free. But she didn't. She elected to take the punishment along with him.

Instead, she accepted her sentencing and continued to write her mother.

"Dear Mum," Myra wrote. "I knew that I would have to go to prison for some time for 'harboring'. But I didn't think it would be for this long. Ian is in prison, in the special wing. Poor thing, he sews mailbags during the day. He says it helps to pass the time quicker than expected. Will you do one thing for me, ma'am? Take out a policy on me or for me, for a half gram a week. I can't even begin to think of the future. It will be something to fall back on."

"Ian has got a little mouse in his cell. He feeds it crumbs and sits in bed watching it nibble them. The other night, he left it half a chip, thinking it wouldn't touch it but when he woke up the next morning it had disappeared."

Over the next three years, Myra would bombard her mother with requests for the photographs of her and Ian together. She said she did this at the behest of Ian who wanted both the slides and photographs desperately. Myra's mother eventually relented by was sure to allow the police copies of the negatives.

"Ian wanted those pictures back so bad because it reminded him of the events," Orange said. "That is the sort of thing we've come to expect from certain types of serial killers. They want to relive the moment in their fantasy. They'll take mementos, pictures, different elements of their crime in order so they can relive it in their minds. The pictures of Myra holding their dog on those burial sites were of paramount importance to Ian."

Myra would die in prison in 2002 of respiratory failure. Her ashes would be scattered over the Moors, a place that she loved so much.

"Was Myra Hindley sick or was she evil?" Entwhistle asked. "She had a violent father. She met a sexually sadistic man who desperately wanted to be a serial killer. All those things came together and made her carry out some evil, appalling crimes."

Ian Brady remains alive, living out his years under suicide watch in a psychiatric facility where he has repeatedly stated that he will kill himself if given the chance.

CHRISTA PIKE

SHEILA DRAYTON

Christa Gail Pike, born 10 March 1976, currently sits on Tennessee's death row for the murder of Colleen Slemmer, 19, on 12 January 1995. The murder occurred when Pike was 18 years old. Pike and her then-boyfriend Tadaryl Shipp who was 17 at the time of the murder were convicted of Slemmer's murder and conspiracy to commit murder. Another friend of the defendants and the victim, Shadolla Peterson, also 18 at the time, was convicted as an accessory after the fact and given six years' probation after turning informant. Pike was sentenced to death by electrocution in 1996 and, at the time, she had the distinction of being the youngest woman ever to be sentenced to death, in any state and only the second women given the death penalty in Tennessee.

Early Life

Pike's life reads like a primer for depraved murderers. As a small child, Pike did not enjoy a healthy and supportive bond with her mother, Carissa Hansen, a licensed nurse, allegedly because of her premature birth. Whereas thousands of children are born prematurely and do not resort to criminal behavior Pike's birth was presented as evidence of one possible origin of her poor and troubled behavior. Pike's maternal grandmother was verbally abusive and Pike was raised by her alcoholic and abusive paternal grandmother until the latter's death in 1988 when Pike was 12; after which Pike attempted suicide by overdosing. She was then shuttled back and forth between her divorced parents' homes. In 1989, Pike was kicked out of her father's house for the second and final time due to her unruliness and the alleged sexual abuse of her father's then-two-year old daughter with his second wife.

Prior to the murder, experts assert that there were myriad indications that Pike was seriously disturbed; however, nobody who may have suspected this sought help for the increasingly disobedient and incorrigible young lady. According to Pike's mother, she was problematic since the age of eight and the two of them had a contentious relationship due to Pike's fluctuating and troubling behavior. Her mother asserted that by age nine Pike was growing marijuana in pots at their home and had been permitted to have a live-in boyfriend at age 14. At one point—in an effort to improve their relationship—Hansen suggested that she and Pike smoke marijuana together. Hansen mistakenly believed that cultivating a friendship with her daughter would cultivate the necessary bond Pike had been lacking her entire life. At one point, one of her mother's boyfriends whipped Pike with a belt which prompted her to wield a butcher knife against him before he was subsequently arrested. Hansen also admitted that Pike had repeatedly lied to and stolen from her. In several interviews with Hansen throughout Pike's trial and seemingly endless appeals, she admitted repeatedly that she was a terrible mother and should have spent more time with her daughter.

Pike's aunt, Carrie Ross, provided insight into Pike's upbringing when she testified that she disallowed her own children from associating with Pike because she lived in a filthy house that had zero ground rules and that Pike was a pathological liar of whom she was somewhat afraid. She also admitted that there was a history of substance abuse in Pike's family. Ross also stated that on the few occasions that Pike actually visited her she behaved like a little girl and engaged in Barbie and dress-up play with her eleven-year-old cousin. Further, there were some allegations that Pike may have been sexually abused but these were neither confirmed nor denied.

Pike's father, Glenn Pike testified that he did, in fact, kick his daughter out of his house multiple times; the last time being in 1989 after the aforementioned allegations that Pike sexually abused her two-year old half-sister. He admitted that he had signed adoption papers for Pike prior to her 18th birthday and that during the times she resided with him she was manipulative, disobedient, and dishonest.

After dropping out of high school, Pike began Job Corps classes in computer programming. Job Corps is a government-based organization that provides occupational and vocational training to underprivileged and troubled teens. It was at the now-defunct Job Corps center in Knoxville where she met Shipp, Slemmer, and Peterson. While Job Corps seeks to promote prosocial behavior and foster a strong desire among its participants to learn a vocation and secure a more promising future than might have been previously the case, this program is also known to cultivate criminal activity, likely due to the association among its participants; many of whom already had problematic behavior.

Evidence of Premeditation

On 11 January 1995, the day before the actual homicide, Pike told friend and co-Job Corps student Kim Iloilo that she was planning to kill Slemmer because she "just felt mean that day." Iloilo discounted Pike's statement as nothing more than merely talk; however, the following evening at approximately 8:00 p.m. Iloilo witnessed Pike, Shipp, Peterson, and Slemmer leaving the Job Corps center. When Iloilo saw Pike, Shipp, and Peterson returning at approximately 10:15 p.m. without Slemmer she, again, thought nothing of it. Even when Pike visited Iloilo's dorm room at 11:00 p.m. that night and confessed to killing Slemmer—as well as showing Iloilo what Pike identified as a piece of Slemmer's skull—Iloilo still failed to tell anyone. Later, at Pike's trial, Iloilo testified that while Pike was iterating the events of the murder she was oddly smiling, singing, and dancing around the room. The following morning Iloilo asked Pike what she was going to do with the piece of skull. Pike nonchalantly replied that she had it in her pocket and was, in fact, eating breakfast with it.

Pike also told another student, Stephanie Wilson, a similar account the following day and proudly described the brown spots on her shoes as blood. Not unlike Iloilo, Wilson failed to immediately report anything.

The Crime Scene

On 13 January, officers from the University of Tennessee and Knoxville Police Departments were dispatched to greenhouses on the

University's agricultural campus in Tyson Park where a University grounds department employee reported finding, at approximately 8:05 a.m., what he assumed to be a dead animal. The gruesome discovery was a corpse that turned out to be Colleen Slemmer. She was naked from the waist up; her throat was cut; her head had been bludgeoned; and she had various cuts all over her arms, throat, and torso—including a pentagram that had been carved into her chest. Officer John Terry Johnson who testified at Pike's trial described Slemmer's body as so badly beaten that she was unrecognizable as a human being. He also stated that he thought he was looking at her face when, in reality, Slemmer was lying face-down in the dirt and debris where Pike, Shipp, and Peterson had left her.

There was additional evidence and testimony that the crime scene encompassed an area that measured 100 feet long by 60 feet wide; an astounding 6,000 square feet in area. Despite the area being muddy and wet there was ample evidence of a physical struggle with trampled bushes, a considerable amount of blood, body drag marks, and hand and knee prints. Thirty feet from Slemmer's body was a large pool of blood which suggested that Slemmer was attacked in one area and then dragged to where her body was later found. Slemmer's shirt and bra were also discovered at the crime scene, as well as a bloody rag that Pike admitted to tying over Slemmer's mouth at one point to keep her from screaming.

Disturbingly, University of Tennessee police officer Harold James Underwood, Jr., who was the officer assigned to secure the crime scene, testified at trial that Pike and a few other females came to the scene between four and five p.m. the day of the discovery and before Pike was even considered to be a suspect. Underwood stated that Pike had asked why the wooded area was marked off, who the victim was, and whether police had any leads as to who the suspect or suspects were. He particularly recalled Pike's odd behavior—moving around a lot while giggling amusedly—and that she wore a necklace in the shape of a pentagram. The following day, during briefing when informed that the victim had a pentagram carved into her chest, Underwood reported Pike's behavior and necklace to his supervisors.

Autopsy and Findings

During Slemmer's autopsy, the medical examiner, Dr. Sandra Elkins, had to identify the victim's body from dental records because her head was so bludgeoned that she was unrecognizable. After cleaning up Slemmer's body which was clad only in jeans, socks, and shoes, and covered with dirt and twigs, Dr. Elkins began cataloging Slemmer's wounds. Due to the sheer number of wounds on her back, arms, abdomen, and chest, and the fact that following department policy which stated that each individual wound be assigned a letter of the alphabet, when Dr. Elkins reached double letters she, instead, individually catalogued only the most serious wounds and that there were innumerable other superficial and defensive wounds. Among the most serious cuts was a six-inch gaping wound across Slemmer's throat that was deep enough to penetrate the fat and muscles in her neck as well as the aforementioned pentagram. Additional injuries included fresh bruising which Dr. Elkins asserted was consistent with crawling.

Cause of death was ultimately attributed to blunt force trauma to the head. Dr. Elkins surmised that Slemmer's head was hit with the asphalt at least four times—two to the left side, one over the right eye, and one to the nose—which collectively resulted in multiple and extensive skull fractures. One of these blows was to the left side of Slemmer's head—which, according to Dr. Elkins, occurred with the right side of the victim's head against a firm surface. This blow only fractured her skull but also imbedded a portion of Slemmer's skull into her head and contained black particles from the piece of asphalt determined to be the murder weapon.

Even more tragic was Dr. Elkins' findings that none of Slemmer's other wounds would have rendered her unconscious and evidence of active blood flow around the wounds and blood in her sinus cavity indicated that Slemmer was alive during the severe torture she suffered before being killed.

Arrest and Confession

The police quickly connected Pike to the homicide thanks to the piece of Slemmer's skull discovered in Pike's jacket pocket. Pike had left this jacket hanging on the back of a chair in Job Corps Orientation Specialist Robert A. Pollock's office on 13 January after meeting with him about a misplaced ID card. Pike's jacket remained in Pollock's office from 4:00 p.m. on 13 January until 7:30 a.m. on 17 January. After learning over the weekend that Pike was a suspect in Slemmer's murder investigation, Pollock immediately gave the jacket to William Hudson, the Job Corps' safety and security captain who turned it over to Knoxville Police Department Officer Arthur Bohanan. At trial, Bohanan would testify that he found a small piece of bone in one of the pockets and presented it to Dr. Murray Marks, a University of Tennessee forensic anthropologist who was reconstructing Slemmer's decapitated skull and the piece in Pike's jacket pocket fit perfectly into an area where a portion of her skull was missing at the time of the victim's discovery.

When confronted with this evidence and subsequently arrested, Pike waived her *Miranda* protections and confessed to the murder and permitted officers to search her dorm room where the blood-soaked jeans she wore the previous night were found. Additionally, Pike led officers to a trash can at a nearby Texaco station on Cumberland Avenue where she had disposed of Slemmer's ID and a pair of gloves Pike had been wearing at the time of the homicide.

Pike's transcribed confession was 46 pages long.

In it, Pike admitted that there was animosity between Slemmer and her because Pike was convinced that Slemmer was a rival for the affections of her boyfriend, Shipp, and that Slemmer was trying to get Pike kicked out of the Job Corps program so she could have Shipp for herself. Pike also claimed that she had awakened one night to find

Slemmer standing above her with a box cutter; however, there is no evidence of this allegation. Instead, Slemmer had repeatedly called her mother, May Martinez, to tell her she was afraid of Pike who she had awakened to find in her room and that she wanted to come home; to which Slemmer's mother said that she couldn't because she had signed a contract. Pike stated that she had only planned to fight Slemmer to stop her from running her mouth. On that fateful night of 12 January, Pike, Slemmer, Shipp, and Peterson signed the Job Corps logbook as they were leaving for an outing Slemmer believed was to smoke marijuana en route to a video store so that Pike and she could try to work out their problems.

When the group entered a tunnel at the edge of Tyson Park, Slemmer likely felt that something was not quite right and proceeded to ask Pike where they were going and whether there was, in fact, any marijuana. These questions irritated Pike who began the brutal assault shortly thereafter after they had gone deeply enough into the woods so that nobody could hear them that led to Slemmer's murder.

Pike confessed to initially slamming Slemmer's head into her knee and then throwing her to the ground where Pike continually punched, kicked, and slammed Slemmer's head into the concrete, screaming, "the bi*ch won't die" and that she wanted "to see [Slemmer's] brains flow." According to witnesses Shipp and Peterson, as Slemmer continued to plead with Pike to stop, Pike got angrier and more brutal. Slemmer offered to return to her Florida home, leave her belongings at the Job Corps center, and not tell anyone what happened; however, Pike became more enraged and yelled at Slemmer to be quiet because "it was harder to hurt someone who was talking to you."

In addition to the savage beating, Slemmer had been cut innumerable times with a box cutter and a mini meat cleaver (that Pike had allegedly borrowed from another Job Corps student) to her torso, arms, face, and back including having had her throat slit six times prior to the fatal blow that resulted from having her head crushed by a piece of asphalt. There was also a pentagram carved into Slemmer's chest; however, Pike asserted that Shipp had done that. Pike also confessed to "just watching Slemmer bleed" when the victim got up and tried to run away. Pike admitted to cutting Slemmer's back: "the big long cut."

After the murder, Pike stated that she and Shipp washed their hands and shoes in a nearby mud puddle to conceal the blood, dumped the box cutter, and Pike returned the meat cleaver to the person from which she borrowed it. This person has never been identified.

The physical evidence and co-defendant testimony suggested that the assault and murder lasted from 30 minutes to an hour and consisted of Slemmer repeatedly trying to get up and run away but was prevented from doing so by the co-defendants who also, as Pike testified, contributed to the physical assault by throwing rocks at Slemmer's head and holding her down so she couldn't run away. Later, Pike would testify that she heard voices in her head overriding Slemmer's continual screaming, telling her that she needed to prevent Slemmer from filing charges against her for attempted murder. Pike also admitted that at one point she thought she had heard a noise and went to investigate it to ensure that they were alone, as well as alleging that during the assault she heard Slemmer breathing in blood and jerking but did not let this assuage her anger as Pike continued her savagery.

Even more troublesome, a police video recorded after Pike's confession shows Pike smiling and providing extensive details about the crime at the crime scene, oftentimes mimicking her actions that evening. Many have said that her demeanor on the recording was eerily similar to that of a little girl who was excited and happy that she had experienced the best day of her life and had no problem talking about the events that transpired, the heinousness of her actions, and how she felt about it all.

The facts of the homicide are not nor have they ever been in dispute, thanks to an abundance of evidence. Pike's confession, and witness testimony at the trial.

Pre-Trial Examination

Prior to her trial, Pike was given a battery of assessment tests and examined by numerous psychiatrists including clinical psychologist Dr. Eric Engum who found her to be extremely bright as evidenced by an I.Q. of 111—in the 77th percentile of the general population—which he believed to be remarkable given her difficult childhood and lack of formal schooling beyond the ninth grade. Dr. Engum also found that Pike had excellent reasoning, problem solving, language, and analytic skills, and was also quite adept at paying attention, sustaining concentration, and sequencing information. Dr. Engum concluded that Pike was legally sane and had no brain damage which has frequently been demonstrated to cause violent behavior in some individuals.

Of particular interest was that Pike was found to be marijuana- and inhalant-dependent and also diagnosed with borderline personality disorder. Whereas there are some similarities between borderline personality disorder and antisocial personality disorder such as impulsivity, irritability, aggression, and a self-image that fluctuates between self-aggrandizement and despair, there are several differences. Individuals with borderline personality disorder differ from those with antisocial behavior in that the former—which primarily affects females—is characterized by a lack of remorse, self-destructiveness, black-and-white thinking, alcohol and/or drug use or abuse, unstable relationships characterized by fear of abandonment and extreme swings between love and hate, difficulty in achieving academic and vocational goals, and are more likely to have been sexually abused; while the latter—which affects disproportionately more males—is characterized by a lack of affect and remorse, emptiness, and an ultimate goal of self-preservation.

Pike demonstrated all of the aforementioned characteristics of borderline personality disorder which makes it easier—but not justifiably so—to comprehend how her intense jealousy of Slemmer and fear of losing Shipp made her commit her atrocious acts. In addition to her fear of abandonment, Pike also abused drugs, was likely sexually abused, had contentious relationships, and displayed zero remorse. Dr. Engum surmised that Pike did not act with premeditation or deliberation in Slemmer's murder but, instead, in a manner that was consistent with borderline personality disorder. More simply, Pike had lost control. However, on cross-examination Dr. Engum admitted that Pike's deliberate luring of Slemmer, that she carved a pentagram in the victim's chest, that she brought weapons with her, and that she bashed Slemmer's head into the concrete does, in fact, constitute deliberateness.

That Pike was overjoyed and singing in Iloilo's room describing the murder while dancing around with the portion of Slemmer's skull Pike had taken as a trophy further supported Dr. Engum's diagnosis of borderline personality disorder because she had eliminated who she perceived was in competition for her boyfriend, Shipp, and, therefore, could continue her relationship with him. When questioned about the piece of skull Pike had taken, Dr. Engum said that Pike had no identity and her actions of taking and displaying the skull was a way to get recognition, no matter how misleading and distorted said recognition might be. In fact, after her conviction and sentencing Pike wrote a letter to Shipp which was intercepted by jail personnel that stated that even though she tried to be "nice" to Slemmer by bashing in her head instead of letting her bleed to death she was still sentenced to "fry."

The Trial

There was an abundance of evidence presented at the trial. Physical evidence consisted of crime scene photographs, autopsy reports, bloody clothing, and the piece of Slemmer's skull Pike had taken as a trophy. With respect to this skull piece, Dr. Elkins presented Slemmer's decapitated skull that was reconstructed by Dr. Marks to explain the victim's injuries. The skull presented at trial was complete except for a portion that was missing on the left side of Slemmer's skull. Dr. Elkins demonstrated that the piece of skull found in Pike's jacket fit perfectly into this spot, much to the chagrin of Slemmer's mother who, in a taped interview, stated that Pike was oftentimes giggling and passing notes to her mother and defense attorney during the trial, not unlike an immature middle-schooler.

At the trial, the State introduced photographs taken of Pike and Shipp at the Knoxville Police Department in which both were wearing pentagram necklaces similar to the shape carved into Slemmer's chest. It was presented that both Pike and Shipp dabbled in devil worshiping and other forms of the occult and that Slemmer was a sacrifice for the next day, Friday the 13th. Despite the presence of some type of satanic elements in Slemmer's murder, Dr. William Bernet, Vanderbilt University's psychiatric hospital medical director, testified that the evidence was that of "an adolescent dabbling in Satanism." He further concluded that the concept of collective aggression—or mob mentality—in which a group of people become stimulated and subsequently engage in some type of violent behavior was most assuredly at play in the events leading to Slemmer's death. However, Dr. Bernet ultimately stated that he did not have enough evidence to definitively surmise whether Pike had acted with premeditation or intent when she lured and murdered Slemmer.

Pike was ultimately convicted of first-degree murder and conspiracy to commit first-degree murder after a mere two-and-a-half hours of jury deliberation. The fact that the jury returned guilty verdicts for first-degree murder—and did it so quickly—demonstrate that jurors were convinced that Pike had the requisite mens rea, or mental capacity, to warrant a first-degree murder charge: premeditation and deliberation. Amidst the overwhelming evidence and utter lack of remorse for her actions Pike was sentenced to death by electrocution (Tennessee has since adopted lethal injection for executions but has the prerogative to utilize electrocution if the lethal injection drugs cannot be obtained). Shipp was sentenced to life without parole because his age at the time of the murder was too young to warrant capital punishment and Peterson turned informant and was given six years' probation for her testimony.

Pike's conviction was upheld by the Court of Criminal Appeals and the United States Supreme Court denied certiorari.

Post-Conviction

While incarcerated, Pike demonstrated more evidence of her depravity. In 2001 she tried to murder fellow inmate Patricia Jones by strangling her with a shoelace. Pike alleges that Jones repeatedly tortured her by calling her "fried chicken" and making various demeaning sounds as an affront to what Jones said was the sound that Pike would make when she was electrocuted. The final straw was when Jones physically threatened Pike's friend, fellow devil worshiper Natasha Cornet. Pike said that she jumped atop Jones and choked her with a shoelace so that the much larger and heavier Jones would get off of Cornet. By the time prison guards reached them, Jones was unconscious.

Pike was subsequently convicted of attempted murder despite her prior death sentence because any offense committed while an individual is incarcerated must be adjudicated. During this time, neurology specialist Dr. Jonathan Henry Pincus began investigating Pike's brain to glean some type of knowledge as to why Pike behaved and continued to act violently the way she did when she assaulted Jones. He asserted that every killer he has ever examined share three commonalities: brain damage, a history of abuse, and mental illness. Dr. Pincus alleged that Pike did, in fact, possess all three features and demonstrates all of the requisite features common to serial killers. There is much consensus among professionals that Pike would likely have been a serial killer had she not been caught the first time.

He also testified at Pike's attempted murder trial that her brain's frontal lobes are not "put together properly"; largely due, he claimed, to the fact that Pike's mother drank while she was pregnant with Pike despite denial of this by Pike's mother. It was also brought up that as a child Pike played at the slaughterhouse where her grandfather worked and that she was frequently subjected to pornography and horror movies on the home television screen. He asserted that all of these factors provide insight into how an 18-year old girl could act with such depravity as was the case when Pike murdered Slemmer. However, the original trial judge, Mary Beth Leibowitz, stated that Pincus' "findings" of brain damage was curious as the defense expert at Pike's original trial who was trying to spare her the death penalty failed to find such evidence.

Forensic psychiatrist William Kenner testified that Pike had suffered from undiagnosed bipolar disorder, the symptoms of which were evident from the time Pike was a "sleepless, talkative adolescent" and likened her to an automobile with cruise control set at 120 miles per hour. Pike's post-conviction defense team alleged that this non-diagnosis justified her requesting a new trial.

In 2002 Pike sought to have her appeal legally stopped and to proceed with her execution. In June of that year Judge Leibowitz granted Pike's request and scheduled an execution date of 19 August 2002. However, a few days later Pike changed her mind and the Tennessee Court of Appeals subsequently stayed her execution. In October 2005, Pike's death sentence was affirmed; however, no execution date has been set at this time.

Pike was again in court in 2007 when her defense team headed by Donald E. Dawson asserted sought a new trial, alleging ineffective assistance of counsel in that her trial defense team failed to introduce evidence supporting Pike's alleged bipolar disorder. During this hearing, Shipp admitted to misinforming investigators and that he, in fact, was primarily responsible for Slemmer's murder. He stated that he was drunk and tired and just wanted the police to leave him alone when he put the onus of blame on Pike. Additional testimony from prior Job Corps student and the defendants' mutual friend Tyrone Comfort stated that Shipp controlled and abused Pike despite her assertions that he was the first male to protect her and she admired the respect and fear he elicited from others. Pike, however, was heavily medicated during this hearing for her alleged bipolar condition and the hearing was rescheduled for April 2008.

During her 2008 hearing, prosecutors portrayed Pike as a cold-blooded vicious killer who not only planned Slemmer's murder but prolonged it for sport, essentially playing cat-and-mouse with Slemmer by allowing her to get up and try to escape and then pushing her back on the ground for additional torture. Ultimately, her request for a new trial was denied.

Pike became newsworthy again in 2012 when she formulated an escape plan with the help of 34-year-old New Jersey resident Donald Kohut who frequently visited Pike in prison but the extent of their relationship remains unknown, and 23-year-old former prison guard Justin Heflin. In a joint investigation by the Tennessee Department of Corrections, the Tennessee Bureau of Investigation, and the New Jersey State Police after receiving information about the plan, both men were arrested and charged with bribery and conspiracy to commit escape, with Heflin charged with an additional facilitation to commit escape charge due to his job as a prison guard. Authorities discovered contraband evidence in the facility which could have only been brought in by a staff member and that Heflin was likely involved. Further investigation demonstrated that Heflin knew Kohut and that Heflin was receiving gifts and money for his assistance in the escape plan. Pike was also charged.

Even more recently, during yet another post-conviction relief hearing in 2015, testimony revealed that Pike was allegedly pregnant at the time of the murder. While this may be true it neither excuses her actions nor provides any potential evidence of legal insanity to justify an affirmative defense of not guilty by reason of mental disease or defect or guilty but mentally ill. Also during this hearing, Slemmer's mother requested the missing piece of her daughter's skull so she could bury the whole of her daughter but was denied as the skull piece remains a critical piece of evidence in Pike's ongoing legal appeals.

Since exhausting the state appeal process, Pike's new defense attorney, Assistant Federal Defender Stephen A. Ferrell, filed a 123-page petition on her behalf alleging that he constitutional rights were violated in both the original 1996 trial and penalty phase and that Tennessee's appellate courts ignored said violations. Among these claims is that capital punishment would amount to cruel and unusual punishment in violation of the Eighth Amendment of the United States Constitution because of Pike's youth, immaturity and mental illness. While Shipp—only 17 at the time of the murder—was too young to warrant imposition of a death sentence, Pike was not. Ferrell alleged that her trial lawyers were incompetent and failed to introduce evidence of mental illness, brain injury, and post-traumatic stress disorder. In response, the state Attorney General submitted a 90-page rebuttal repeatedly asserting that the state courts' ruling were all legally correct. As of the beginning of 2016, this battle continues.

Numerous video interviews of Pike over the past several years show her admitting that she was fully cognizant of her actions and that they were wrong. She stated that she felt as though she was taking out years of abuse on Slemmer and that she committed a horrible atrocity and deserves to be punished; however, she asserts that she deserves life without the possibility of parole for her actions; not the death penalty for the actions of three individuals. She has repeatedly stated that she wishes it was she who died and not Slemmer but such protestations are moot after the fact. One cannot help but wonder if Pike actually means what she says or is simply saying what she thinks others want to her. Knoxville Police Department detective Randy York who worked the case has said that in his lengthy career he has not encountered many people who he believes are evil but that Pike is, indeed, the personification of evil and that she should never be permitted to be around other human beings ever again.

Experts assert that the death penalty is not an effective general deterrent and debate over the morality and legality of capital punishment remains contentious and in the forefront of public discourse and debate. Currently, Tennessee is only one of 38 states which have the death penalty. Whereas women comprise 13% of those arrested for murder, only 2% are sentenced to death and, of those, only 3% are actually executed; primarily due to judges not wanting to sentence women to death. In Tennessee, only two individuals on death row have been executed—both males. The last time a woman was executed in the state was in 1837. Many currently believe that Pike will likely never be executed.

MANSON'S GIRL : THE TRUE STORY OF LYNETTE SQUEAKY FROMME

CHAD TROTTER

Lynette Squeaky Fromme

Covering the tragedy of the Sharon Tate and LaBianca murders of the late 1960's, this book documents the twisted spiral of Lynette "Squeaky" Fromme. This book explores how the relatively normal world of Californian suburbia that Lynette Fromme was born into could lead her into the arms of the most notorious cult leader and cult group in history. Taking into consideration how the warped beliefs of a street hustler named Charles Manson could have such a pull on her and the rest of the Manson Family. Come along with us as we explore Fromme's role in the crime and times of Charles Manson and how this troubled young woman would eventually make an assassination attempt on the life of a United States President. She was an average American girl but something, somewhere along the way went terribly wrong. This book attempts to answer the question; what happened to Lynette Squeaky Fromme?

Introduction: What's the Problem?

The year was 1967. The war in Vietnam was just heating up, the Civil Rights movement was fully mobilized, and protesters were arriving en masse in opposition to the conventions of the day. But even with all of the political axes to grind, in 1967, the 18-year-old "Squeaky" Lynette Fromme was just a lost little girl wanting to find a way back home.

When the ex-convict and aspiring cult leader Charles Manson found her, she was weeping on a bench, depressed and frightened after her latest go round with her authoritarian father had left her homeless and on the street. Manson who—of all things—had taken coursework in prison that was based on the motivational book "How to Win Friends and Influence People" already knew how to win friends and he certainly could influence people.

Manson had finely honed his powers of manipulation and his ability to read others all the way back in his Juvenile Hall days in Indianapolis, Indiana. He developed a great capacity to infer what those around him wanted to hear and see, and then copiously worked to give them just that, as he constantly worked over his guards, attorney's and even court judges with his concerted efforts at charisma.

Seeking to be a heavily refined conman, it was a skill that seemed to serve Manson well, allowing him to charm his way through the parole board on several occasions. It was on his latest get out of jail free card excursion that he found Lynette Fromme drowning in her own tears on that public bench. And knowing exactly what to say, without any pretense or hesitation he instantly inserted himself in this troubled young girls world and cut through everything she was feeling so ill at ease about, by simply asking the question, "What's the problem?"

Chapter 1: The Family Business

The day Lynnette Fromme met Charles Manson she began a lasting partnership with the convict turned mystic. In truth, she became one of his first followers in what would become the "Manson Family". The group of free love drug addicted misfits who flocked to Charles Manson's promise of an alternative society. Manson often called himself the "Gardener" and fancied himself a caretaker for all of the misfit flower children of the 1960's who wandered his way.

The wacky beliefs that Manson expressed to his followers in the scorching hot heat of Death Valley were as laughable as they were stupidly offensive. Even worse than his wacky beliefs, however, was his inane ability to pull perfectly good rock music down into the derelict dumps with him.

Dropping acid and listening to Beatles records was one of Manson's favorite pastimes, and it was in the midst of this hobby of his that he somehow became convinced that the Beatles were prophets who had chosen to speak directly to him through coded messages in their music.

And the message that Manson fixated more than anything else, was the one he believed to have gleaned from a song called, "Helter Skelter" which Manson somehow believed to foreshadow future civil unrest and even ethnic cleansing. Shortly after the bloody murders in which Manson's brainwashed followers had scrawled the same two words on the walls with their victim's own blood, it would be Helter Skelter that would become the Manson Family's calling card.

Helter Skelter had become so associated with Manson and his crimes that it eventually forced former Beatles John Lennon and Paul McCartney to weigh in on the controversy. They really didn't know how Manson could have developed such a bizarre interpretation of their song.

Lennon contended that the title "Helter Skelter" was taken from an amusement park that had stood across the street from one of the venues they had played. The lyrics were really just a running gag reflecting the rides at the park with lyrics like, "When I get to the bottom I go back to the top of the slide, where I stop and I turn and I go for a ride."

Both John and Paul have always asserted that Helter Skelter never had much of a deep meaning at all, it was just the band getting together and playing a goofy, silly song. But for Charles Manson's disturbed mind it was some sort of twisted revelation. And as Charlie's loose associations with rock music and prophecy continued, his group of devoted followers, including one Lynnette Squeaky Fromme, became just as convinced as he was.

Convinced that the apocalypse was nigh, the Manson Family's original plan was to just wait it out in their own little commune in the middle of Death Valley, while society destroyed itself and then wait for the traumatized remnants of the civilized world to come crawling to them in the desert. Because who would the shattered remnants of civilization seek out to rebuild the world? Why Charles Manson of course.

It's all pure, unadulterated, tripped out insanity that makes as much sense as the paranoid schizophrenic who believed David Letterman was communicating to her through her television set. But for all of Charles Manson's insanity, he had a powerfully insidious charisma that had crept over his followers, and Squeaky Lynnette Fromme soon believed every warped word out of the madman's mouth.

And so it was that Lynette Fromme's new family spent the rest of the 1960's out in the desert waiting for the end of the world to arrive. But the end of their world didn't come in the form of societal collapse, the Manson Family's world would come crashing down around them when they were implicated in the murders of actress Sharon Tate and a couple name Labianca.

Even though his followers and Manson himself always contended that Manson had never actually killed anyone with his own hands, it was quickly believed that the twisted cult leader had inspired his followers to kill on his command. And in the aftermath of Manson's incarceration, it was Lynette Fromme who became his number one advocate, tirelessly showing up at court hearings, dictating his will and testament and incessantly speaking to reporters.

But much more than this, she quickly became the mouthpiece and the de facto leader of the Manson family in Charlie's absence. For the media at the time, it seemed that if Charles wasn't in charge, then well, Lynnette Squeaky Fromme most certainly was. The most well-spoken member besides Manson himself, Fromme quickly became a main focal point of media attention. According to Manson attorney Paul Fitzgerald, it was Lynnette who expressly formed the Manson Family's "heartbeat".

And for a time, even without Manson, Lynnette Fromme and many of her former Manson Family sister's tried to carry on, even recruiting more men who might serve as a surrogate for Manson. Lynnette attempting to emulate her hero preached to drifters and the discontented. But when men heard the words of Charles Manson's philosophies coming out of Lynette Fromme's mouth they often fell flat or seemed more like an offbeat form of amusement than any kind of real alternative in life.

Fromme would try her best to emulate Charles when she spoke of how the women's liberation movement had undercut American men disrupting the order, but when she spouted things like, "American women were wearing the pants, they had taken their men's balls and chained them up" something that would have had converts nodding along if they came from Charles Manson, just came off as absurd, offbeat, drunken humor when they came from petite little Lynette Fromme.

But while Fromme tried to secure her grip on the family, many in Charles Manson's legal team were attempting to secure their grip on Fromme. Manson's main defense attorney, "Paul Fitzgerald"insisted that Fromme was key to defending the case against Charles Manson.

And he began frequently meeting with Fromme, eventually designating her as a material witness in the case.

This was a move happily welcomed by Fromme since it meant that she would finally be able to visit the incarcerated Charles Manson. Fitzgerald meant to use these meetings as constructively as he could in order to bolster his defense, but much more than legal strategizing, for Lynnette Fromme these meetings usually turned into her own debriefing sessions for the family's former head.

Charles would prod her for information about the latest happenings with the family and then before she left, he would give her hundreds of commands and special assignments to carry out on the outside. If he wanted her to contact someone, she would, if he wanted her to discipline another family member she would, Fromme was now Manson's last window into the outside world and ultimately his messenger to the rest of the family and whoever else he wished to speak to.

But all of these seemingly obscure tasks, suggestions, and assignments that Fromme would receive from Manson none of them proved to have anything at all to the case at hand and attorney Paul Fitzgerald grew increasingly disconcerted. But as erratic as Fromme may have seemed, there was one area in which she always served to benefit the defense team and that was in bringing public awareness to the case.

From the beginning, Fitzgerald figured that the only way they could beat the system and win a not guilty verdict for Charles Manson would be to turn public opinion against the legal process itself. And in this task, Lynne Fromme was a ceaseless cheerleader. She once famously announced, "There is no love in that court, no God in the machine—just a lot of big words that swear to God and stagnate life, rather than adjusting justice, they make the court into a gladiator ring."

In her own jumbled and disjointed way, Fromme was making her own case to the public that the courtroom was like a modern arena in which men like her own modern day Spartacus; Charles Manson, were pitted against odds that were purposefully stacked against them. Fromme felt that if she could espouse this unfair treatment to the public she just might be able to shift the balance in Manson's favor.

So Fromme went on her own Charles Manson awareness campaign, and all over California she would proclaim to anyone who would listen, "Come to the trials—your trials—and see what's going on." This publicity campaign did manage to generate interest. And even if it was just out of morbid curiosity, people did come, so much so, that every courtroom seat was filled, and even outside the packed courtroom, curious onlookers crowded the scene.

But as the courtroom began to overflow with observers Fromme soon found herself without a seat of her own. The prosecution detesting the circus that had been created and viewing Fromme as a distraction would not allow her to attend. Since Fromme and her other acolytes were not allowed in the courtroom they decided to take their message to the street.

Practically every single day of the trial they would assemble on the corner down the street from the Justice Hall. Their antics became so much of a spectacle that they themselves became a morbid kind of tourist attraction. With people coming from miles around just to see Fromme and these other strange women who tried their best to keep up the family business.

Chapter 2: The Conviction of President's

For President Richard Millhouse Nixon, 1970 was proving to be an interesting year. The United States had just invaded Cambodia, greatly escalating a war Nixon had pledged to subdue, inflaming protests at college campuses all around the world. Just one month prior to this signing, 4 young protesters had been shot and killed by the National Guard at Kent State in Ohio. And then, of course, there was the ongoing trial of Charles Manson. A media circus that Richard Nixon freely commented upon on August 4th of 1970 when he declared in regard to Manson, "Here is a man who was guilt, directly or indirectly, of eight murders without reason."

Manson's guilty verdict made headlines across the national media the next day. One of the attorneys had brought a copy of of one of the newspapers to the courtroom proceedings that day, and Charles Manson seeing it, went berserk and snatched it up off the table, holding up for all to see Nixon's condemnation of him. Manson's efforts proved to be part out of outrage and out of cunning manipulation. Manson and his followers hoped that Richard Nixon's biased conviction could grant him a mistrial.

And sure enough, the next day, loyal Manson followers took the cue, and asked the judge, "Your Honor, the President said we are guilty, so why go on with the trial?" But trial judge Charles H. Holder was steadfast in his own conviction and suggested that Manson had brought the controversy on himself and then declared the attorney who brought the newspaper in the courtroom was in contempt of court for violating the order against newspaper publications being present during proceedings.

Lynnette Fromme who had already developed a cultivated hatred of the American Justice System was especially affected by Richard Nixon's pronouncement. She now felt it was clear that the system and even the very President of the United States were out to get them. This was a belief that she maintained and nurtured even after Nixon's replacement by Gerald Ford and many contend that this was what planted the seed of her desire to assassinate President Ford. She wanted to get revenge for the wrong she thought Richard Nixon had done them.

Manson himself tried to throw the President's conviction right back at him, when he declared in reference to Richard Nixon, "Here's a man who is accused of murdering hundred of thousands in Vietnam, who is accusing me of being guilty of eight murders." But no matter how Charles Manson tried to spin it, the proceedings would be destined to continue.

And now a new element of the case against Charles Manson began to merit the concern of the Manson followers; the prosecutions new star witness, former Manson Family member Barbara Hoyt. Barbara was a reluctant witness and had been pressured early on to testify. Wishing to hide from the whole affair she had contacted Lynne Fromme and other former family members, seeking advice as to where she could lay low.

Lynne and her cohorts then came up with the idea that she should fly to Hawaii with two other family members so she could avoid her court date. Apparently, Barbara initially agreed to the plan and flew to Hawaii with the two other members. It was here that Barbara began to have second thoughts, however, about whether or not she should truly avoid giving her testimony.

But before she could decide which way she was going to go with it, one of the member's gave her a hamburger drenched with enough LSD to send someone into a complete psychosis. Shortly afterward Barbara was found collapsed in the street mumbling about her courtroom duties to the lead prosecutor, stating, "Call Mr. Bugliosi and tell him I won't be able to testify today in the Sharon Tate trial."

Known as the "hamburger plot" Lynne and her others were quickly apprehended with charges of conspiracy and obstruction of justice. The lead prosecutor Vincent Bugliosi then did his best to convince the court that Lynn and her compatriots wanted nothing more than Barbara to either die or become permanently disabled from an overdose of LSD. Although the more serious charges were later dropped, Lynne Fromme and her cohorts were all hit up with a "conspiracy to dissuade a witness and conspiracy to bribe a witness" and thrown in jail.

It was from the depths of the Sybil Brand Correctional Institution for women that Lynnette Fromme was summoned once again to stand trial as a witness for the Manson defense team. During her testimony, she proved to be quite a burden for the Judge who had to snap her to attention and keep her on track with several yells of "Just answer the question, Miss Fromme".

From the outset, Fromme seemed more interested in using the witness stand as a platform from which to proclaim her views and the Manson family values than any recognizable form of usable testimony for the defense or the prosecution of a murder case. Growing increasingly frustrated, Judge Older soon silenced her words and ordered all counsel to a impromptu meeting with him in which he told Fromme's defense attorney, "this witness is not interested in being responsive to the questions asked her" and informed him in no uncertain terms that Fromme was not to, "use this court as a forum for her philosophies."

Whatever Lynn was trying to accomplish with all of her statements, it was to no avail, however, and all of the defendants charged with murder received an unequivocal pronouncement of death, while Lynne Fromme herself was quietly shuffled off to the Sybil Brand Institute for Women to serve the rest of her conspiracy charge. For most of America, the case against Charles Manson and his family was closed, but for Lynette Squeaky Fromme it was only beginning.

Chapter 3: Life outside the Pen

When Lynnette Fromme was released from the Sybil Brand Institute for Women in the year 1971, it seemed as if the whole world had changed; at least the world of Squeaky Fromme that is. Charles Manson was sitting on death row along with the other Manson Family members who were charged in the Tate and LaBianca murders. But for Fromme, it seemed that it was more than her friend's lives that had received a death sentence because it was her idealistic dreams—dreams that she had shaped with her fellow Manson family members—that seemed forever condemned to death as well.

The world she came back to was now unrecognizable, completely drained and empty of everything that she had previously hoped for. The summer of love which had flourished in Haight Ashbury with all of its promises was now lost forever. And the man who she looked to as a brilliant and wise father, the man they called the "Gardener" in the hopes that he could cultivate their minds for spiritual growth, was now forever ingrained in everyone else's mind as nothing more than a psychopathic killer.

When Fromme hit the streets after her release in 1971 she found a world gone cold that she no longer recognized. Most of her previous contacts had either disappeared or no longer wanted anything to do with her. For the rest of the year, Lynnette Fromme would bounce around from place to place and spend most of her energy writing a book about Manson which she hoped would somehow convince the world of his goodness and grant him a pardon.

Of course, none of this happened. Even when she finally finished her rambling monolog the story was so radioactive, even with the lure of media attention, no publisher was willing to touch it. Meanwhile, the legal system, or as Fromme and her colleagues frequently called it, "The System" seemed to be moving further and further away from them. As was made evident on October 21st, 1971 when Richard Nixon nominated the conservative Judge William Rehnquist to the Supreme Court.

But even so, Lynn still held out hope for a reversal of Manson's fate, one way or another and as a part of this, she started to establish her own contacts in the legal scene. One major part of this was her introduction in the Spring of 1972 to an up and coming San Francisco Attorney by the name of Doug Vaughn. A notorious figure in the region who drove a pickup truck and often sported a strangely Country Western look replete with hat and cowboy boots.

Lynnette maintained a rather superficial relationship with Vaughn and with him found sympathetic ears as she railed against the government she felt so betrayed by. Vaughn recalls one instance in which the topic came to the latest Democratic candidate for president, George McGovern, a conversation that led Fromme to make the blanket statement about politicians, "They're all just a bunch of liars and crooks."

But speaking of crooks it was soon Lynne Fromme who would develop a whole new cadre of crooks, liars, and thieves, who would ultimately implicate her in another notorious murder. Under the influence of Charles Manson who had forged a partnership with the prison gang, "The Aryan Brotherhood" a fresh flood of ex-cons came flooding into the Manson Family world.

During the course of these events, two of Lynne's friends were killed by the gang members and Lynne herself once again guilty by association was rounded up and thrown in jail once again as a result. It was here that her newly established legal consultant Doug Vaughn came to Lynette's rescue. After Vaughn investigated the case he discovered that the charges leveled against her had no weight.

From the police reports, he determined that the only reason the police brought her in was because she had hung out at the suspect's house and of course because of the tremendous reputation she had as the defacto leader of the Manson cult that already preceded her. The police had just hauled her in based on all of that. Lynn would finally have all charges once again dropped on January 2nd, 1973 and released back out on the streets of California.

Her freedom would not last long since the LAPD had a deep suspicion that Fromme had been involved in a robbery at a Seven-Eleven back in October of the previous year. And after being released from one prison system she was simply shipped off to another one, but in yet another amazingly ridiculous turn of fate in the annals of the Manson family, the "X" Lynn had first carved in her face years ago so that she would be spared from the wrath of locusts, managed to help spare Lynnette from serving another jail term.

Because after Vaughn had the witness to the Seven Eleven robbery take a look at the telltale mark, the witness finally conceded that the person she saw did not have such an unforgettable feature. A few days later the actual woman that robbed the store was captured and after she confessed to the crime Lynne was once again released to live life outside of the Pen.

Chapter 4: The Making of an Assassin

With her own legal battles finally settling down Lynette Fromme was struggling to find her place in the world once again. She was living off of $90 a month on welfare and found room and board at another cheap flat. Even though her surroundings were meager, and her outlook seemed bleak, many thought that she was finally trying to move on with her life and leave the Manson Family behind her.

But as fate would have it, a bestselling book would send her scrambling right back into the arms of extremism. Released in November 1974, Vincent Bugliosi published his book "Helter Skelter" which described the events that had become so infamous with the same working title. Fromme was still hurt over the fact that she could never get anyone to publish her own book, and then to find that someone else had beaten her to it was frustrating.

And then when she actually read the book for herself she was incensed to find certain passages that described her own presence and character in ways she found very upsetting. In one passage Bugliosi even seemed to call into question her mental capacity as he described Lynette Fromme and Sarah Good, "as if they hadn't aged but had been retarded at a certain stage in their childhood."

There it was for the whole world to see; Lynnette Fromme was mentally retarded, irrevocably stunted by Charles Manson who had snatched her up at 18 years old and warped her brain beyond recognition. This outrage spurred Lynnette Fromme to try once again to get her own book published so she could in her own words, "effectively combat the Bugliosi thought syndrome" and she now became utterly obsessed with telling her side of the story.

Meanwhile, President Nixon had resigned in disgrace and was replaced by Gerald R. Ford as the new President of the United States. Despite the seat change, however, it didn't take long for Lynette Fromme to redirect all of her anger at the "system" and Nixon, firmly on the linebacker shoulders of President Ford. She would tell a journalist at the time, "Ford is picking up Nixon's footsteps, and he is just as bad."

Donning her new cult uniform of a red robe Fromme then set out to shut down all of the ills that she claimed had been caused by government bureaucracy from Ford on down the line. One day she barged into a cement factory and demanded them to stop production because it was hurting the environment. In another instance, she even wrote a scathing letter to the Prime Minister of Japan criticizing him for Japanese Whaling.

At this point, calling herself a "Nun of the Earth", Fromme had given up men and embraced the environment, all the while claiming that she was ready to eliminate anyone that polluted the Earth. Even though many of her proclamations were startling with their degree of menace and violence, most people still did not take the petite form of Squeaky Lynette Fromme seriously.

In 1975 she heard that President Ford, the current embodiment of all her perceived evil was coming to town. It was an alignment of events that she just couldn't resist. Fromme remembers how disgusted she was with the excitement of everyone around her that the President was coming. Incensed with what she viewed as a gross and false form of adoration. At the time she intoned to her friend Sandra Good that President Ford was "a dummy, an empty head" and that his adoring fans were, "like sheep looking up to this dead head with dead thoughts."

With increasing rage and hatred that the whole city would turn out to see this "dead head" of a man, Lynette Squeaky Fromme determined that she would be the one to finally silence the object of her hatred once and for all. On September 5th, 1975 waiting with a crowd of, as she would put it, "adoring sheep" Lynette Fromme was the wolf in sheep's clothing, besides the brilliant red crimson of her dress she just looked like a small, pleasant-faced woman, waiting to see the President.

But when he came within just a few feet from Ford, as he was blithely shaking the hands of onlookers, President Ford saw Fromme move toward him out of the corner of his eyes. Ford assumed that she just wanted a presidential handshake as well, but when he stopped to look at the woman, instead of an extended hand to greet him, he saw a gun in his face instead.

After a momentary look of panic, President Ford scrambled to get out of the way of the deranged woman's line of sight, while Secret Service Agent Larry Buendorf screamed the ominous warning, "forty-five"!

Acknowledging the Colt Forty Five that the strange figure in red was waving in her hand Buendorf then pounced on Fromme and ripped the weapon from her hands as a seemingly puzzled and disappointed Fromme cried out, "It didn't go off!" For some reason the gun had failed to fire, granting a sad and dejected Lynette Squeaky Fromme yet another item to her growing list of failure.

Conclusion: Hiding From the Past

By the time of Lynette Fromme's attempted assassination of Gerald Ford, she had actually been quite used to getting arrested, being shuffled through the system and then ultimately being released. She had after all been found implicit with murder on two separate occasions already, and each time she was released.

And so it was that when her gone had failed to go off, preventing her from assassinating President Ford. Squeaky was subdued and believed that her charges would be dismissed since she "caused no harm."

But whether Fromme realized it or not, due to federal legislation enacted shortly after the assassination of President John F. Kennedy, assassination attempts came with a mandatory sentence of life in prison. But as much as she hated the system it would smile on her eventually, and she was released after just 34 years of her sentence in 2009.

Meanwhile, Charles Manson and the other family members are still in prison. Their death sentences were commuted when California abolished the death sentence, but they will no doubt be behind bars for the rest of their lives. But what about Lynnette Squeaky Fromme? Where is Lynnette Fromme now? The last anyone knew she was dodging the media, avoiding the limelight for a change, and trying to avoid anything and everything to do with her past.

BLACK WIDOW JUDY BUENOANO

57

ERIN CARTER

Judy Buenoano loved men. But she loved killing them more.

In 1971, she murdered her husband James and nine years later she would kill her own son, Michael. In 1983, she would attempt but fail to kill her boyfriend, John Gentry. She is also believed to have been responsible for the death of Bobby Joe Morris (another boyfriend) in 1978. She was never convicted of the Morris crime, however, as by the time the authorities had connected the dots she was sentenced to death for the murder of her first husband.

But the suspicions didn't stop with the Morris death. Buenoano is also suspected of killing a man in 1974 and in 1980, another boyfriend would die under suspicious circumstances.

Buenoano would become the first woman executed in Florida since 1848 and only the third woman executed since capital punishment had been reinstated in 1976.

She would be sent to the electric chair in 1998. Her last words were that she wanted to be remembered as a "good mother."

Instead, she would go down as one of the most sadistic female serial killers in American history.

This is her story.

EARLY LIFE

Judy was born Judias Welty in Quanah, Texas on April 4th, 1943. Her father was a day laborer at a local farm. Judy would talk about her mother being a full-blooded member of the Mesquite Apache tribe but little did she know that a "Mesquite Apache" tribe didn't exist.

Her mother would die of tuberculosis when Judy was only two years old. She and her baby brother Robert would be sent to live with their grandparents while their two older siblings would be put up for adoption.

"When Judy's mother died," forensic psychologist Paula Orange said. "It sent Judy's life into a tailspin. This is one of those 'Butterfly Effect' scenarios. A tragic circumstance that occurred early in a child's life that led to her perpetuating pain on everyone else for the rest of her own adult life."

She would eventually leave her grandparents and join her father in Roswell, New Mexico. He had remarried and Judy would claim that both he and her new stepmother would beat, starve, and burn her with cigarettes.

They made her a "house slave", forcing her to do chores around the house at their bidding. Judy would finally act out at the age of fourteen as she would burn two of her step brothers with hot grease. Not stopping there, she attacked both her father and step-mom with fists flying.

Police would be called and Judy would be jailed for over two months. After she served her jail time, the judge gave Judy a choice, either return home or go to reform school. She opted for the latter and was sent to Foothills High School. She would remain there until 1959 when she would graduate at the age of sixteen.

She held her entire family in contempt, particularly her younger brother Robert.

"I wouldn't spit down his throat if his guts were on fire," Judy once said when asked about her brother.

CHANGING IDENTITY

Judy returned to Roswell but changed her name to "Anna Schultz". She found work as a nurse aide and would give birth to a baby boy out of wedlock, Michael Schultz on March 30, 1961. Judy would remain silent on the identity of the baby's father but people believed that Judy was having an affair with a pilot from the nearby air force base.

In 1963, the twenty-two-year-old Judy would marry James Goodyear. Goodyear was twenty-nine years old and serving as a sergeant in the United States Air Force.

They would have their first child together, James Jr, four years later. James would celebrate the event by legally adopting Michael. Daughter

Kimberly would come a year later as the family would move to Orlando, Florida.

Judy would then open her own business, starting the Conway Acres Child Care Center in Orlando. She listed James as the co-owner even though he was during a one-year tour in the Vietnam War. After returning home, he only had three months of downtime before he was admitted to the U.S. Naval Hospital in Orlando, complaining from symptoms staff physicians never quite identified. He would die on September 15, 1971.

Goodyear was only thirty-seven years old at the time of death and authorities believed he died due to natural causes.

"He came home from Vietnam ill and he never got well," Judy said. ``It had nothing to do with me. I was not in Vietnam."

"Crazy that Goodyear was able to survive the horrors of Vietnam but not Judy Buenoano," Orange said. "He had no idea he was married to a sociopath. She had no respect for the fact that he had just put himself on the line for her and the country. All she saw were dollar signs."

Judy poisoned James with arsenic and waited almost a week after his death before cashing in his three life insurance policies. A few months later, an "accidental fire" burned down their Orlando home. Judy would receive another $90,000 in fire insurance.

She lost her husband and her home. But her purse was never fatter.

NO GRIEVING WIDOWS ALLOWED

Judy would waste no time finding another man. Despite having three kids in tow, she would find a new love in Bobby Joe Morris when she moved her family to Pensacola.

It was business as usual for Judy as she had a fat bank account courtesy of James Goodyear and a new beau in Bobby Joe. Eldest son Michael, however, was not doing well in school. He scored on the low end on IQ tests and was a behavioral problem. Judy would get him evaluated at a state hospital in 1974 and then sent Michael out to foster care where he would also receive psychiatric treatment.

Judy's new home would suffer another "accidental fire" and she collected money from the insurance. She then took Michael out of foster care and moved to Trinidad, Colorado with Bobby Joe and the rest of her children. Judy then changed her name from "Anna Schultz" to "Judias Morris".

FOUR YEARS MAX

Judy would date Bobby Joe for four years before deciding it was time to cut him loose.

Bobby Joe would start to suffer from the same mysterious illness as James Goodyear did years earlier as he complained of dizziness and vomiting. He would be admitted to San Rafael Hospital on January 4, 1978, but doctors would not be able to pinpoint what was wrong with him. He would be sent home to Judy's care two weeks later. Two days later, however, he would would pitch face-first into his dinner plate, unconscious. He would be rushed to the hospital, but Judy knew that her "medicine" had taken effect.

Five days later, Bobby Joe Morris would be dead. Doctors would chalk up his death to cardiac arrest and metabolic acidosis.

Judy would wait, just like she did after she killed James, before cashing in on Bobby Joe's life insurance.

Authorities were none the wiser.

But Bobby Joe's family suspected something fishy was going on. Back in 1974, Judy and Bobby Joe had been visiting Brewton, Alabama when a man from Florida was found dead in a motel room in that town. Police would find the man in the room after receiving an anonymous call. He was shot in the chest with a .22-caliber weapon and his throat was cut open.

Judy's connection to the crime? Bobby Joe's mother had overheard Judy telling her son about the murder.

"The sonofabitch shouldn't have come up here in the first place," Judy said. "If he came up here he was gonna die."

Bobby Joe had told his mother about the crime on his deathbed. She thought the confession could be attributed to his delirium, but Bobby Joe told her too many specifics to ignore.

"We should never had done that terrible thing," Bobby Joe mumbled to his mother. "Never should have done that to him."

She tipped off police but they would not be able to find any fingerprints inside the room and no bullet was recovered from the corpse. The case remained unsolved.

WHAT'S ONE MORE SURNAME?

On May 3rd, 1978, Judy would change her name again. This go around, she would change her last name to Buenoano, which in Spanish meant "good year." She stated that she meant it as a tribute to her husband James Goodyear and her Apache mother.

Things continued to go bad with Michael as he dropped out of high school in the tenth grade. With limited employment opportunities, he would join the army in June of 1979 and get assigned to Ft. Benning in Georgia after basic training. When he was on his way to his new post, he visited Judy in Pensacola.

Judy greeted her son with open arms. Then she began poisoning him.

By the time he reached Ft. Benning, he felt sick. Army physicians would find seven times the normal level of arsenic in his body.

They could do little to reverse the damage done. Six weeks after his arrival, the muscles in his arms and legs and deteriorated to the point where he was a paraplegic.

"Michael had no use of his legs," Orange said. "And he could not move his arms past his elbow. Again, Judy was a sociopath. It is unfathomable for a normal human being, a mother, to do this to her own child. Yet she did it to Michael. He was always an inconvenience to her but now that he had military insurance he could become an asset in death."

Judy would give Michael the short shrift while favoring James and Kimberly. Michael and James didn't get along well as clearly their mother favored the latter. Judy would hide Michael when people came over because she was ashamed of him. She would have a neighbor named Constance Lang watch over him when visitors arrived.

"Michael didn't fit the picture Judy wanted to present to the world," Orange said. "She wanted to be looked at like a woman of high status. She drove a Corvette and owned her own business. Michael was a slow-thinking kid. She didn't want anyone to see that."

The army didn't investigate the reasons behind Michael's inordinate levels of arsenic. Instead, they set him up with leg braces and a prosthetic device on one of his arms.

He would be discharged from active duty because of the medical disability.

But his mother saw dollar signs.

The day after his return home, Judy wasted no time. She organized a fishing trip with Michael, James, and daughter Kimberly. They would leave Kimberly ashore at the East River bridge while they went into the water with a two-seat canoe. A small folding lawn chair had been placed in the middle of the canoe for Michael who had was outfitted with a leg brace, a fishing reel, and a ski belt.

James would state that had fished for about two hours when they were reaching shore when a "snake fell into the canoe." He said that everyone panicked as the snake slithered around. The canoe hit a log and capsized.

James would claim to have been knocked out by the impact and would remember nothing until he came to inside an ambulance.

He would tell this version to the court but when he was talking to Army investigators, he made no mention of a snake.

"There is conjecture as to how much James was involved or much did he know," Orange said. "The statement given to the army investigators is different from what he would state later in court. The statement given to the army was a written statement and the handwriting didn't seem to match his own."

A man named Ricky Hicks saw the overturned canoe, an ice chest, and a plastic bag in the river. He also saw Judy and James.

"I lost the other boy," Judy said as Ricky approached them on the shore. "A snake had gotten into the canoe and I tried to hold the snake down with a paddle."

"Where is he?"

"It's no use," Judy said, waving him off.

Hicks said Judy appeared to be concerned about James then asked him for a beer. He then drove Judy's car to a nearby phone and called the county rescue squad.

The rescue team arrived and began looking for the missing Michael.

The canoe had not moved as there was barely a current. They would find Michael's body one-quarter of a mile upriver where the canoe had been rescued. The rescuers stated that it should not have been a problem to swim upstream, suggesting that Michael could have been saved.

Judy initially said that Michael had a life jacket on but later recanted and said that it was a ski belt.

There was no ski belt on Michael when he was found.

Judy would later state that after the canoe capsized, she saw James lying face down in the water. She swam over and cleared his air passage to resuscitate him. She looked around for Michael then was picked up by Ricky Hicks.

"Michael disappeared under water," Judy said. "I went to rescue James. I almost lost both of my sons that day. Mothers just don't murder their children. If I'd have lost both of them, I don't know what I would have done. They would have had to put me in a mental institution."

"Kimberly's boyfriend would later testify that Judy had killed Michael for the insurance money," Orange said. "The children knew about their mother but she had clearly brainwashed them into silence. She provided for them, she fed them. She knew what was best."

Telling the police that she was a "clinical physician", they bought her story of the boat capsizing. The army investigators did not buy her account. Not having any evidence, however, they would eventually pay her Michael's military life insurance ($20,000). Investigators got suspicious, however, when they found out that two civilian life policies were taken out on Michael. The applications on both policies look to have been forged.

Judy's former sister-in-law, Peggy Goeller, would call to inquire how she was doing. She would make no mention of Michael's death during her first call but on a second call she told Peggy that Michael had died "during Army maneuvers".

MOVING ON

Judy would demonstrate very little grief over Michael's death and she would not be charged with his murder. Foremost on her mind was finding another man and another big check.

She opened a beauty salon in Gulf Breeze and found her next mark: businessman John Gentry.

Gentry was more well-heeled than her previous conquests so Judy put on airs for his sake. She told him that she had Ph.D.'s in biochemistry and psychology and was the former head of nursing at West Florida Hospital.

Gentry believed her story and decided to spoil his blue-blooded girlfriend expensive gifts, vacations and the finest cuisine all in the name of courtship.

Pushing the envelope, Judy would encourage John to provide life insurance for both them both. She then secretly boosted Gentry's coverage from $50,000 to $500,000 without him knowing.

Two months later, Judy began giving Gentry "vitamin pills".

"Come on," she said, placing two pills into Gentry's palm.

"What are you, my mother?" Gentry asked.

"Well, God forbid I want to see you healthy," Judy slid the cup of water toward her prey.

Gentry would then complain of dizziness and later begin vomiting after his daily dose of Judy's "vitamins."

He would admit himself into the hospital and noticed that his symptoms disappeared when he stopped taking the vitamins.

Still smitten by Judy, he did not suspect her of wrongdoing. Instead, he took her vitamins and hid them in his briefcase.

One night, however, Judy sat him down for a special dinner. She had a very special announcement.

"I'm pregnant," she said, smiling in triumph.

"Finally," Gentry said. He told Judy that they should celebrate. She told him to go to the liquor store for an expensive bottle of champagne.

"Be right back," he said, kissing her with excitement.

Running out the door, Gentry got into his car and a bomb exploded with he turned the ignition key.

Amazingly, Gentry survived the blast as trauma surgeons saved his life.

"Judy really overplayed her hand with the explosion in the car," Orange said. "Really it speaks to her level of dedication and ingenuity. Who knows where she got the idea, maybe watching the Godfather. But the police found the dynamite residue inside Gentry's car. They decided to look no further than to Judy herself."

Their interrogation and research would unearth lie after lie. They found out about the $450,000 increase in Gentry's life insurance.

Gentry himself thought the insurance had been canceled. He was shocked to learn that she had increased the payout and was paying his premiums out of her own pocket. The police didn't spare him any quarter. They would him that she was not a real doctor and that she couldn't get pregnant.

"What?" Gentry muttered, completely flabbergasted.

Judy had been sterilized seven years earlier.

Gentry couldn't believe his ears. Police would go on to say that she had booked tickets for a world cruise for herself and her children...leaving Gentry out. They discovered that Judy had been telling her friends that Gentry was suffering from a "terminal illness."

The only "terminal illness" Gentry had was Judy Buenoano.

Now fully convinced, Gentry would reach into his briefcase and give police the "vitamin pills" that Judy had been giving him.

"Judy was emptying the vitamin casing and filling it with formaldehyde and a little arsenic," Orange said. "Over time, this would have been lethal."

The state attorney would refuse to charge Judy as they wanted an air tight case in order to prosecute. Knowing that they had their killer, officers, and federal agents searched Judy's home in Gulf Breeze, obtaining wire and tape from her bedroom that looked to match the same wire/tape they found on the bomb in Gentry's car.

They would search her son James' room, finding marijuana and a sawed-off shotgun. He would be jailed him for possession of drugs and an illegal weapon.

"Again, this is a strange mistake on Judy's part," Orange said. "She was meticulous and a good liar. Why she didn't remove any and all evidence from her home is a head-scratcher. She had gotten sloppy because she had gotten away with so many crimes before without so much as a slap on the wrist. She thought she was above the law, got careless and left incriminating evidence behind."

Judy would then be arrested at her beauty salon and charged with attempted murder. It took a month of police work, but authorities would trace the source of the dynamite used in the bomb, linking the Alabama buyer to Judy via phone records which showed numerous long-distance calls from her home.

Judy would pay bail but authorities would not let up. Five months later, she would be indicted for first-degree murder in the death of her son Michael, with an additional count of grand theft for the insurance scam.

Feeling the noose around her neck, Judy would fake a seizure and wind up in Santa Rosa Hospital.

Authorities then exhumed the bodies of the men they believed she killed. Bobby Joe Morris was exhumed with arsenic found in his remains. Identical results were obtained with the exhumation of James Goodyear, in the following month.

Connecting the dots, police obtained a court order to exhume the bodies of all the men that had died while associated with Judy; son Michael, husband James Goodyear, and boyfriend Bobby Joe Morris.

Arsenic would be found in all of the bodies.

"There was enough arsenic in him (Goodyear) to kill twelve people," Detective Ted Chamberlain said. "So he was loaded. I mean that boy was loaded with it when he went down."

OPEN AND SHUT CASE

In 1984, Judy would be convicted of the murders of Michael and attempted murder of Gentry. In a separate trial in 1985, she would be convicted of the murder of James Goodyear in which she would ultimately receive the death sentence.

Judy would be imprisoned in the Florida Department of Corrections Broward Correctional Institution death row for women.

HER FINAL HOURS

Judy would spend her last day watching a hunting and fishing show, eating chocolates, and talking about old times with her children and cousin Jeanne Eaton. She would read a suspense novel called "Remember Me" and her last meal with be steamed broccoli, asparagus, strawberries and hot tea.

Judy's impending execution did not receive the same media attention as Karla Faye Tucker whose was executed only a month earlier. Her execution was opposed by the Pope and Jesse Jackson.

'"She may not have been as photogenic, as young or as pretty as Karla, but she was just as good a Christian," Eaton said.

"Judy obviously had her enablers within her family," Orange said. "How could she be 'just as good a Christian' if she is poisoning people, blowing them up and the 'Christian' she is being compared to is ice-picking people to death. People say the strangest things."

But Judy herself was bitter that no one paid much attention to her presence on death row, particularly the fact that she was a woman.

``Karla was a young female, very attractive and she had become a Christian in prison," Judy said. ``We all prayed that she would be granted a stay of execution and clemency because we felt that she was a different person and she deserved a chance. Possibly, I am a different person. But I was a Christian when I came here. I was a devout Catholic. I've not changed in that."

"It was a bit of a curiosity as to why the media was so charged to prevent the execution of Karla Faye Tucker and paid little heed to Buenoano," Orange said. "Tucker's killings were ferocious and sadistic while Buenoano's killings could be seen as passive. But what drew people to Tucker was her physical appearance and demeanor. She came across as a sweet, reformed choir girl at the end. She had a charming smile and a soft voice. Buenoano, on the other hand, looked sinister. She had squinty eyes, high cheekbones and a snarling, Southern drawl. Her body language and demeanor screamed hostile."

Judy would enter the death chamber with several guards by her side. They strapped her into the large oak chair, placing leather straps over her waist, wrists, chest, and legs.

They fitted the calf and headpiece electrodes last, inserting a wet sponge in between to reduce the burning of Judy's skin.

"Do you have a final statement?" the warden asked.

"No, sir," Judy closed her eyes tight.

The witnesses on the other side of the glass partition watched in silence.

Judy did not look at them as a leather mask was placed over her face.

The warden nodded his head and the switch was pulled.

Steam wafted up from her right leg as her body jolted for thirty-eight seconds. Her hands balled into fists, white knuckling from the shock as smoke rose from her feet to the ceiling.

Then Judy went limp. She would be pronounced dead at 7:08 a.m., March 30th, 1998.

The date was her son Michael's 37th birthday.

KILLING FOR MONEY

71

SANDRA WINSTON

"Anna was flat broke. But when she saw a person walking down the street she would think that individual had HER money in their pocket. If she had to kill that person to get HER money, then she would take out her poison and say 'let's get this party started.'" - forensic psychologist Paula Orange

Anna Marie Hahn had a gambling habit.

She indulged her addiction at the horse races and bookie joints throughout Cincinnati in the 1930s. Anna wasn't very good at picking horses, losing time and again while accruing debt.

But it was an addiction had to be fed.

She needed a scheme, a way to acquire money to keep her compulsion satisfied.

Anna Marie Hahn was a clever woman. While walking through her neighborhood of elderly pensioners, the idea came to her like a bolt of lightning.

She would befriend these lonely and pathetic men. Cook them meals, keep them company.

Then she would kill them for profit.

EARLY LIFE

Anna was born Anna Marie Filser on July 7, 1906. She would be the youngest of twelve children born to a well-to-do Catholic family. Nothing in her childhood would suggest that she would eventually become a serial killer. She was never abused sexually or physically.

Nonetheless, she had suffered a few concussions during her childhood years during ice skating, biking and skiing adventures. These head injuries may have attributed to altering her personality as sometimes been the case of some serial killers. Anna also stated that she was a sickly child, suffering from blood poisoning, goiters, and scarlet fever. It is her belief that these instances led to "her mind changing that she could do the things that happened."

As a teen, she had given birth to a son named Oskar out of wedlock. The identity of the father has remained shrouded in mystery to this day although some claim a Viennese doctor had seduced Anna Marie.

She never revealed who the father was as he was a married man who wanted her to abort the child. Anna felt "just like a mountain was falling on top of her, not killing her but just smothering and crushing her."

The pregnancy brought shame to Anna's family. They sent pregnant seventeen-year-old to live with a sister in Holland until the baby was born.

She would return to Germany afterward and remain there for five years. The shame of being a single mom in a conservative, judgmental society would prove to be too much for Anna to bear.

"I could no longer stand those things that people were saying about my misfortune," Anna said. "I was afraid that my son would understand those things. These things were hurting my mother who was caring for my boy."

"Back in the day," Orange said. "Having a baby out of wedlock was the worst thing a woman could do in terms of family legacy. She had humiliated her entire family and was banished to another country. It certainly is an antiquated notion now, to shame a woman for having a child out of wedlock and it has become the norm. In Germany, however, this act was cause for ostracization."

Anna left Germany and arrived in the United States on February 12th, 1929. She had a step-uncle who lived in Cincinnati to whom she had written a year earlier. "I want to come to the United States," she wrote. "I'll repay you if you can lend me money for the trip. I will have little trouble finding work as a housekeeper. Please write back."

Her step-uncle, a seventy-four-year-old retired carpenter, was impressed with Anna's ability to provide for herself once she arrived. She did so well, in fact, that he became suspicious of how she acquired her money.

Oskar would stay behind in Germany with her parents while Anna would live with her now expatriated relatives Max and Anna Doeschel. Growing accustomed to the American way of life, she would meet another German immigrant named Philip Hahn at a dance. Philip was immediately smitten by the blonde and buxom Anna. The courtship did not last very long, a few weeks of dating was all the convincing Philip needed to ask Anna to marry him.

Anna agreed to marry him only on the condition that she be allowed to bring her son from Germany to live with them. Philip consented and the two were married three months after their first meeting on May 5th, 1930, in Buffalo, New York. Two months later, Anna would return to Germany and bring back Oskar who was now six years old. Philip would work as a telegrapher and do his best to now provide his new family.

Wanting a better life for her son, Anna convinced Philip that they should do more. The Depression was in full bloom but that did not stop Anna and Philip from starting their own restaurant and then a bakery. Both ventures would prove to be economic failures. The two soon became bankrupt and were forced to move in with a childhood friend of Anna's father.

Thus marked the continued humiliation of Anna. Branded as a whore by her own family, she was shunned and banished to America where she would suffer the indignity of becoming bankrupt.

GERMANS IN CINCINNATI

There was a sizable German population in Cincinnati and Anna was able to fit in and find friends. She settled in a community called Over The Rhine and she was welcomed with open arms.

She repaid some of these new "friends" by killing them.

"She had it all," author Diane Britt Franklin said. "She knew how to manipulate, steal, poison."

But what prompted her to turn to murder?

The friend of Anna's father had left his home to the Hahn's but they still had a mortgage to pay. Philip lost his job as a telegrapher, a victim of both technology and the Depression. The walls started to close in on the couple as creditors began making threats to take possession of her home.

Anna did not know what else to do.

So she turned to gambling.

Three years into her marriage, Anna was neck-deep in debt because of her gambling habit. She loved the racetracks but could never pick a winner. She would play horses at the Blade, a bookie joint in suburban Elmwood, Ohio then the gaming tables in Newport.

The addiction grew faster than her pocketbook would allow.

She needed money. Fast.

So she found a new way to "earn" money. Unbeknownst to her husband, Anna began plotting ways to pilfer money out of elderly German men who lived in Over the Rhine.

She developed a method typical of male serial killers in that she had a typical victim. Anna thought long and hard about what type of man she should target. The lonely. The old. The German, with whom she would be able to ingratiate herself to.

Anna found an apartment building in Cincinnati that was comprised mostly of older German men.

They were the perfect foil for Anna Hahn. A young and beautiful German woman who spoke their language, they easily fell prey to her charms.

"She went through apartment buildings," Franklin said. "She knocked on doors and asked for old men who were single."

"She developed a method of extracting money from wealthy old people," Orange said. "She would gain access into their homes by offering her services as a nurse. Then she would take their money."

Ernst Kohler was believed to be her first victim. Anna had befriended the lonely German man and he had willed his house to her.

Getting the sense that she was onto something, Anna began "befriending" more elderly men. The next victim was seventy-two-year-old Albert Parker who enlisted Anna's aid as a caretaker. Anna would borrow over $1,000 from Parker and signed an I.O.U for it. After Parker's death, the letter of debt "disappeared."

SETTING THE STAGE

Anna dressed her son in his Sunday's best before they went prospecting for victims. The little boy wore a brown suit with a beige shirt and a derby hat. Anna dressed conservatively, looking like a German mother taking her son out to Sunday School. She wore a gray jacket with a black silk blouse. But Anna made sure that her silver cross necklace stood prominently over her cleavage.

She then knocked on the apartment door of Jacob Wagner and put on her best smile.

Th door creaked open and the elderly German man peered out at them, saying nothing.

"Mr. Wagner," Anna said in a strong German accent. "I'm Anna Marie."

The old man's face brightened with good cheer. He had a young woman to help around the house with chores.

Little did he know that Anna would help herself to his bank account and personal belongings.

"She would take a nickel as easily as a dollar," Franklin said. "She would steal anything in sight."

Jacob Wagner was a retired gardener who only had a few thousand dollars in savings. He was targeted by Anna who would tell his neighbors that she was his niece. The old man became confused, responding back that he had "never heard of her."

"Neither Jacob nor the rest of the community fully realized what a psychopath Anna was," Orange said. "If you had something she wanted, whether it be money or material goods, she would do anything in her power to obtain it. If it meant killing you, so be it."

Anna knew that she only need to apply her feminine wiles on Wagner and he would be putty in her hands. She told the old man that she was an heiress to $15,000 from Germany. She wanted to pool their resources to buy a chicken farm but in the meantime would working around his apartment.

The seventy-eight-year-old Wagner would die on June 3rd, 1937, only months after hiring Anna. The day after the gardener's death, Anna would go to Wagner's bank and present a check that was made payable to her. The bank asked her about the death of Wagner, she had conceded that she had forged the check. Anna would not stop there. She would appear before a probate court with a will that left all of Wagner's property to her.

She had forged out a will but didn't realize that Wagner never developed the ability to write in English.

"I hereby make my last will and testament," Anna wrote on behalf of Wagner. "I am of sound mind and no influence. I have my money in the Fifth Third Union bank. I want my funeral expenses paid and all my bills. The rest I leave to my relative, Anna Hahn of 2970 Colerain Avenue, who will be the executor of my estate. I want no flowers and I do not want to be laid out. (Signed) Jacob Wagner."

She would steal his money to pay off her gambling debts. But the addiction would not go away.

Anna simply could not stop herself from gambling.

She would go to the racetracks up to four times a week and her losses once again began to accrue.

"Anna was very smart when it came to selecting the right victim and circumstance," Orange said. "But she was too stupid to realize that she wasn't very good at picking a good horse. She had a compulsive personality disorder. Anything that she saw had a positive benefit would be repeated over and over again. She became good at getting into the graces of older men and taking their money. So that became another addiction that she had to feed."

MORE LONELY OLD MEN

Anna would meet another elderly man in the mostly German neighborhood. His name was George Heis. She would arrive at his home and entertain the old man with her charm and gaiety, making drinks for him as he sat on his couch.

"Mr. Heis was a coal dealer that she met and befriended," Franklin said. "She got very friendly with him. He would take the money he would collect from his coal deliveries and give it to her."

George lived it up with Anna, drinking up the best bourbon and laughing it up in his living room.

He didn't know that Anna was counting the days when she would kill him.

One night, she would lace his drink with arsenic. He would remain paralyzed for the rest of his life.

"Arsenic loves to attack the endothelial cells," Orange said. "Those that line the blood vessels. When it attacks, those blood vessels begin to leak. Leakage of blood anywhere, particularly in that central nervous system, can cause symptoms such as paralysis."

Heis drank Anna's poisonous concoction and immediately began gasping in pain. He stood up and staggered around the room.

Anna simply watched as the old man's eyes bugged out as he tried to make it to the bathroom.

"She was heartless," Orange said. "She would watch the old man stagger in front of her, begging for help. Her only response would be to take a sip from her own drink as he collapsed to the ground and writhed in pain."

Anna would not stop with George Heis. She continued to poison men and the community was none the wiser.

"Yeah, all these people were dying in this close-knit community," Franklin said. "And no one was saying a word. Eventually, someone spoke up and said 'Hey, we're missing one.' And they reported it to police. The police didn't believe it. They didn't have any evidence to go on and they would just slough it off."

The coal company began to inquire with Anna for the money she owed Heis. She had to find a new benefactor and found one in Albert Palmer, a retired railroad watchman who had a small pension. She would meet Palmer at the Blade, the gambling joint where Anna frequented. Palmer became smitten with the youthful Anna who wrote the lonely old man love notes, calling him, "my dear, sweet Dady" (sic) and would sign her notes to him "with all my love and kisses, your Ann."

"I wrote like that," Anna said," because I regarded him like a father."

Anna would borrow money from Palmer which she used to pay off the coal company. Anna had provided company to Palmer and cooked him "homestyle German meals." Palmer was smitten by Anna but not so smitten that he didn't want his money back. Anna then took care of the debt owed to the old man by giving him a nice helping of poison in his mashed potatoes.

Palmer then became ill and died on March 27th, 1937.

CATCH ME IF YOU CAN

Anna was getting away with murder with no end in sight.

"Even today, you don't suspect a woman of being a serial killer," Franklin said. "They're not that many. But maybe there are a lot more than we think because they're hard to detect. They're very hard to detect. Who would suspect a nice German lady like Anna Marie Hahn of being a serial killer? You just would not believe it and the police didn't either."

Anna was able to avoid detection because of her ability to think rationally and plan out her attacks. Unlike some of her fellow serial killers, her murders were not done on the spur of the moment. They were cold and calculating with Anna waiting for exactly the right time to execute her victim.

That next victim would be sixty-seven-year-old George Gsellman.

Lonely and pathetic, he nonetheless jumped at the chance to have the young German beauty as his caretaker. She waited on him hand and foot, cooking his meals and cleaning up around the house. Her son would also quickly befriend the sickly Gsellman whom she was slowly poisoning with arsenic and croton oil.

Anna would use the croton oil in order to flush the arsenic out of the system. The oil would cause almost immediate vomiting and on its own could cause death if the victim is not properly re-hydrated.

Anna would take Gsellman for all that the old man had. He would eventually die alone in his room.

"Anna's appetite to get what she wanted had no limits," Orange said. "She wanted that money. Needed that money. That being said, she probably enjoyed the rush of taking someone's life. You don't do something like that for so long without a psychological payoff of some kind. Anna kept killing men not only for profit but because she liked it."

THE DEATH OF JOHANN OBENDORFER

"2150 Clifton Avenue was the home of Johann Obendorfer," Franklin said. "On street level is his little cobble shop that Anna Marie walked into one day because she had broken her heel while out shopping. He fell in love with her but she had other designs. Can you imagine how happy he must have been to have snared this beautiful woman? Little did he know that in two weeks he would be dead."

Obendorfer was the typical lonely widow that Anna would target. She entertained his affection for her by telling him that they should go to Colorado and live on a ranch.

Obendorfer agreed. Accompanied by her son Oskar, Anna would travel with the elderly Obendorfer to Colorado.

But they never bought a ranch together.

Within one day of their arrival in Denver, Obendorfer became deathly ill in his hotel room after Anna gave him some food. He was taken to Bethel Hospital and Anna registered him as being from

Chicago. "I didn't have any money," she said. "I didn't want to be responsible for any bill."

"By the time they got to Denver," Franklin said. "Mr. Obendorfer had gotten very, very sick. She had been poisoning him the whole trip."

She would deny knowing Obendorfer to the hospital staff. They inquired for some identification of the man and Anna leaned over her benefactor on his death bed.

"Old man," Anna said. "Tell these people your name. Tell them who you are."

Obendorfer could not even manage a whisper, he was so weak.

"I don't know who he is," Anna said, throwing her hands in the air. "He's just an old German that I met on the train."

Anna then left the hospital and felt that she wanted more out of the trip that what she was stealing from Oberdorfer. Prepping to leave town, she had one more heist in mind.

"The hotel owner had rooms right behind the registration desk," Franklin said. "One day Anna Marie walked right into one of those private rooms. She saw two diamond earrings on the dresser and stole them. When the hotel owner realized they were missing she filed a complaint with the police in Colorado Springs. By that time Anna Marie and her son had left town and left poor Mr. Obendorfer on a slab in the morgue."

An autopsy would reveal high levels of arsenic in Obendorfer's body.

While Anna was away in Colorado Springs, the police in Cincinnati had finally become suspicious of Anna. They searched her house and found some incriminating evidence.

The police would search through one of her purses and find a salt shaker with enough arsenic inside to kill off all the inhabitants of a small town. They also found a bottle of croton oil that was marked with the words "poison." They found a bottle which contained more than seventy grams of arsenic lodged between the rafters between the cellar and the first floor.

Upon returning home, Anna would be confronted by the police. They would interrogate her about the poison and Anna would deny ownership of the contents but want it back nonetheless.

The police chief at the time, a man named Hayes thought that his intimidating questions would force Anna to crack under pressure.

"There are an awful lot of men dying around you, Mrs. Hahn."

"I love to make old people comfy," Anna said. "It isn't my fault that all these old men are dying. I know it is very peculiar, but why pick on me, Chief?"

"We searched your place, Mrs. Hahn," Hayes said. "We found enough poison to kill half of Cincinnati."

"I have been like an angel of mercy to them. The last thing that would ever enter my head would be to harm those dear old men."

TIGHTENING THE NOOSE

Anna would visit a physician named Dr. Vos whose office was in a building Annie owned and occupied. The doctor would soon discover that many of his blank prescription forms were missing. Anna's husband Philip would come forward with a bottle of poison and inform police that Anna had, in fact, stolen the prescription forms. She would forge the doctor's signature and order the poisons from the local pharmacist.

"She would send our twelve-year-old son, Oskar, to get the prescriptions. One pharmacist refused to fill the prescription because of the boy's age."

Philip then told police that Anna had tried twice to insure his life for $25,000 but he had refused to sign off. After his refusal, Philip began to become ill with the same symptoms as some of Anna's previous victims.

Philip's mother demanded that she take her son to the hospital where it was revealed that he was being poisoned. He recovered but never spoke to his wife again.

With the evidence provided by Philip the police now had enough to arrest Anna Marie Hahn.

On August 10th, 1937, Anna would be placed behind bars.

"She got too cocky," Orange said. "She would leave behind too many clues, in particular with Obendorfer. She forgot to cover her trail and the police eventually got her on their radar. The irony was that the predator, Anna, now became the prey of the police as they spent months gathering evidence on her."

Anna would plead not guilty to the charges of murdering Gsellman. She claimed that she didn't know the man. But a friend of Gsellman told the police that they had witnessed Anna visiting the old man the night before he died.

The investigation grew in scope as the deaths of five other old men and another couple had all died without warning but with one thing in common.

They all were friends of Anna Marie.

THE TRIAL AND EXECUTION

"It took me a long, long time to find that it is wrong to be good to people," Anna said to a reporter outside her trial. "This doesn't mean I am going to be hateful from now on because that is against my nature. They can take a human's body, but they can't take their soul because that will go where there is justice."

When her case went to trial, it shocked a nation that had never seen a female serial killer before.

During the trial, newspaper reporters described Anna as "poker-faced, blonde German woman who at no time displayed any appearance of resentment or shock at anything that has been said."

The prosecutor in the case spared Anna no mercy.

"In the four corners of this courtroom are four dead men," he bellowed. "These men are pointing their bony fingers at this woman as they say, 'That woman poisoned me. She made me die in agony. She made me suffer the tortures of the damned. Let my death not be in vain.'"

The defense attorney argued back that the evidence against Anna was circumstantial and that she was a "victim of a cruel sequence of coincidence."

"What was shocking to everyone," Franklin said. "Was that the jury returned a verdict of guilty without mercy."

The jury would be comprised of eleven women and one man. The prosecuting attorney felt that if the jury was comprised of a male majority they would see Anna as a sympathetic figure. So they stacked it in favor of females.

The guilty verdict meant that Anna would be the first woman in Ohio history to be sentenced to death in the electric chair.

Anna still had enough charm and wit to play on the sympathy of people.

"The judge cried," Franklin said. "Because he had to sentence Anna Marie to death. He had no choice."

"At the end of the day, Anna proved to be like most every other serial killer," Orange said. "She thought that everyone else was beneath her in terms of intelligence. They don't think they can be caught and the vastly underestimate the scope and IQ level of the people around them which include the police. Anna thought she was more cunning that everyone around her. For awhile, she was. Then the noose tightened around her neck and she had nowhere to go."

The night before her execution, Anna would sit down and write out a twenty-page confession of all of her murders. She tearfully described every detail in the small journal, addressing it to "Dear Lord."

"On one hand, you can look at her confessional as a letter begging for forgiveness," Orange said. "But women like Anna aren't remorseful without a payoff. Cold and heartless, she wanted to remain in control until her final breath. Her confessional letter was yet another attempt at control. She wanted to be in charge until the very end."

"I do not show my feelings," Anna wrote. "My troubles in life, starting when I had my baby, had taught me how to control my feelings…I don't know what made me do it. All that I can say is that my troubles were so big that it must have turned my mind. I do not try to excuse myself or my actions. They were not me at all…It all seems like a horrible dream…I wanted to cry out that they were trying the other Anna Hahn and not this one sitting in the courtroom…Maybe it would have been different if I had only told my lawyers the truth. My lawyers fought so hard for me. But that is all over now…I do not fear my end and my last concern is only for my boy. I have written this confession with the full knowledge that death is near and I only ask one favor and that is that my son should not be judged for the wrongs that his mother may have done."

The sale of Anna's confession to the newspapers allowed Anna's attorneys to take care of Oskar's future. They moved him away from Cincinnati and had him placed under a new name. Her husband Philip would remarry shortly after the trial.

There are competing reports of how Anna behaved as she waited to be executed. Some reports describe her as pleading to see her son for one last time. Others describe her as mocking that report, sarcastically asking "do I look like someone who is distraught?"

Nonetheless, before being executed Anna pleaded for mercy. She had reached out to Ohio Governor Daley to grant a stay of execution.

"This was one of the most difficult decisions I've ever had to make," Governor Davey said. "Something inside me sort of rebelled against the idea of allowing a woman to go to the chair but the crimes committed by Hahn were so cold-blooded, so deliberately planned and executed that I have no choice but to permit the decision of the court to stand.

I feel sorry for her son, Oscar, but his mother has bequeathed him nothing to be proud of."

Anna would be sent to the electric chair on December 7th, 1938 at the Ohio Penitentiary in Colombus, Ohio. She refused to see her husband and son on the last night of her life but allowed reporters covering her trial a farewell party. Several of the newsmen entered Anna's cell. She had fruit punch and cake prepared for them.

"You gave me a 'good show' at my trial, boys," Anna said. "The least I could do was to throw a bash for you. I guess I'm not much like a 'beautiful blonde' now, huh? Well, give me a good write-up when it's all over."

THE ELECTRIC CHAIR

"Don't do this to me!" Anna screamed at the prison attendants who began strapping the electric belts to her leg. She writhed against the grip of the guards as they held her down, strapping her to the chair.

Anna screamed in mercy. A priest entered the room just as the black death mask was placed over her head. Her screams and pleas became inaudible.

"Our Father, who are in heaven," the priest said.

Anna could be heard repeating the prayer until the execution flipped the switched as the heavy jolts of electricity crackled through her body.

She screamed for mercy then continued the Lord's Prayer.

"But deliver us-"

Those were her final words.

It took two and a half minutes to kill Anna Marie Hahn on the electric chair.

"Did she protest her innocence to the last?" a news reporter asked her attorney, Joseph Hoodin.

"I won't comment on that," Hoodin said.

"But did she admit her guilt?"

"I understood the question," Hoodin said. "And I still won't comment."

Anna would be buried at the Mount Calvary Cemetery in Cincinnati, Ohio.

BLONDE BUTCHER : The True Story of Ruth Judd

ERIN SPENCER

In 1931, Winnie Ruth Judd killed two of her best friends then cut one of them into pieces. She packed their remains inside two storage trunks and boarded a train for Los Angeles with the dead bodies as "luggage".

The media circus surrounding her crime was a parallel of the O.J. Simpson case in the mid-1990s. Reporters and readers alike were hungry for every sordid detail. Ruth, as she was known to her friends, would be tried and sentenced for execution until being declared mentally incompetent. She would later be remanded to the care of the Arizona State mental hospital where she would "escape" over seven times. During her last escape, she would journey to northern California where she would adopt an alias and avoid detection for over six years before her recapture.

CHAPTER ONE – EARLY LIFE

Winnie Judd was born Winnie Ruth McKinnell on January 29th, 1905. Born in Oxford, Indiana, her family soon moved from town to town as her father preached in different Methodist churches.

She suffered from tuberculosis as a child and was sent to an Arizona sanitarium for care. It was there that the seventeen year old would meet a thirty-seven year old physician named William Judd. They two would marry and Ruth would accompany him to Mexico where he was employed as a medic for American silver miners.

William, a World War I veteran, became a morphine addict in trying to cope with his injuries. The addiction soon seeped into his business life and he began having trouble holding down a job. The couple returned to the United States and began moving from city to city. The marriage was not a happy one as Ruth could not produce children and had repeated bouts with tuberculosis while William continued to struggle with his morphine addiction.

By 1930, the couple had a "needle separation", living apart but still remaining on talking terms. Winnie who had usually been called by her middle name, Ruth, had moved to Phoenix, Arizona where she hoped the drier climate would help with her tuberculosis. She had found work as a nanny to children with the Leigh Ford family, who were well-to-do. Upon her arrival in Phoenix, she met John "Happy Jack" Halloran, a successful businessman.

Halloran was married but was known for having open affairs.

John Halloran was nicknamed "Happy Jack" by the press when they got wind of his philandering ways. He was the co-founder of Halloran Bennett Lumber Company. A jowly man with a jovial personality, he used his wealth and status to procure young "party girls" despite the fact that he was married.

The two met while Ruth worked as a nanny for the Leigh Ford family. Jack lived next door with his wife and spotted the frail but pretty Ruth sitting on the Ford's front porch. He engaged the young woman in conversation and found out that her husband was away at a rehab center fighting another bout against his morphine addiction. Ruth confided to Jack that she was lonely and the opportunistic philanderer made his move.

They affair began on Christmas Eve of 1930 up until the night she murdered Anne and Sammy who were also involved with Jack.

Winnie would quit her job with the Ford family and obtain work as a medical secretary at the Grunow Medical Clinic in Phoenix.

It is here where she would befriend Agnes "Anne" Leroi, an x-ray technician and her roommate Hedvig "Sammy" Samuelson.

The two women had moved to Phoenix from Alaska as they wanted a better climate after Sammy had contracted tuberculosis.

The trio would have a tumultuous friendship that hinted of a love triangle between Annie, Ruth and Jack as well as a hints of homosexuality.

CHAPTER TWO – A TRIANGLE OF LUST

Ruth become close with Annie and Sammy, often having sleepovers at their bungalow. The two women soon become friends with Jack who, being the philanderer that he was, quickly indulged in relations with Annie.

This didn't sit well with Ruth who mistakenly believed that Jack loved her.

On October 16th, 1931, neighbors heard screaming coming from the bungalow. But the yelling stopped as quickly as it started and no one reported the fracas.

"I had introduced Jack to a girl they (Annie/Sammy) objected to," Winnie said in a jailhouse interview. "That is what the quarrel was over. He (Halloran) was a friend of my husband but he was trying to kiss my behind my husband's back. And I loved my husband very much."

Ruth had shot both women in a jealous fit with a .25 caliber handgun.

She then dismembered Sammy's body and put her head, torso, and lower legs into a shipping trunk while placing her thighs in a traveling suitcase. Annie's body was not dismembered, instead being stuffed into another shipping trunk.

The morning after, Ruth showed up late for work at the clinic while her co-workers wondered about the whereabouts of Annie. Later at the trial, some workers reported seeing Ruth as having a bandage on her left hand. Some remembered it being on her right. Others didn't remember it at all.

After her shift ended, Ruth called a moving van to retrieve a pair of large trunks and have them placed on a train for Los Angeles two days after the murders.

Ruth boarded the Golden State Limited passenger train at Phoenix's Union Station with both the trunk and suitcase which contained the bodies. She arrived in Los Angeles but her trunks immediately brought suspicion as porters saw the "stained fluid" coming from the trunks which was emitting a foul smell as well.

The porter, a man named Arthur Anderson, confronted Ruth.

"Ma'am," the porter said. "There's something leaking out of your trunk."

"Is there?"

"You know, a lot of folks try to transport contraband into Los Angeles," the train agent continued. "I've seen it all. Had one big game hunter use his wife to transport a dead deer. You wouldn't do something like that would you?"

"God, no."

"Do you have the keys for the trunk?"

"Its in my car."

"Let's open it please."

"My car is just outside," Ruth said, heading out of the depot. "Just wait right here. I'll get my keys, unlock the trunk and then I'll see what's leaking."

Ruth's younger brother Burton arrived in his vehicle to pick her up. Burton, a USC college student, had no idea that Ruth just committed murder.

"Drive," Ruth commanded.

"Where's all your stuff?" Burton asked.

"Just drive, Burton! Don't ask any questions, just go."

The car sped away as Anderson stepped out of the depot. He had the presence of mind to memorize the license plate of the vehicle and immediately reported the incident to the Los Angeles Police Department.

The police arrived, picked the locks on each of the trunks and were shocked to discovered the dead bodies inside.

"I was the chief investigator of the case," retired Phoenix detective Charles Arnold said. "From the police department in Phoenix at the time it happened. At the time it happened, the Phoenix police department knew nothing of Ruth Judd. Never heard of her. Until our police chief, that morning, received a call about nine o'clock, received a call from the captain of homicide from Los Angeles. The chief had said that they had discovered these trunks with nude bodies in them at the depot."

The police traced the car to Ruth's brother but the woman herself had disappeared. Ruth had gone home with Burton then hid in a department store among other places.

CHAPTER THREE – THE TRUNK MURDERS

The horrific crime would send shock waves throughout the country. The press would refer to Winnie as "Tiger Woman", "Blonde Butcher", and finally the case became known simply as the "Trunk Murders."

On Monday, October 19th, 1931, the Phoenix police force entered the home of Agnes and Sammy. Neighbors and reporters were also on the premises, disturbing the crime scene. The next day, the landlord of the bungalow placed an advertisement in two newspapers informing the public that he would be doing tours of the crime scene for ten cents per person.

Because of the ad, hundreds of people came through the bungalow out of morbid curiosity.

With their forensic evidence now contaminated, police nonetheless believed that both Annie and Sammy were shot while asleep in their beds. Both of their mattresses were missing from the bungalow but one was later found in a vacant lot a few miles away with no blood on it. The other mattress remained missing.

Police would also find a letter that Ruth had written to her husband but never mailed. The letter described a multitude of sexual goings-on at the Phoenix bungalow. Ruth would detail straight, bisexual and homosexual trysts that the trio would engage in.

With his wife now a wanted woman, Dr. William Judd put forth a public appeal for his Ruth to turn herself in.

Winnie caught word of her wanted status and would meet with police on October 23rd in a Los Angeles funeral home.

Detective Arnold led the interrogation of Ruthie as they spoke to her in the funeral home.

"Mrs, Judd, don't you think if a doctor amputated these bodies he would have known where to cut them and had to cut four and five places to find the joint?" Arnold asked.

Ruth shifted in her seat. "Well, it wasn't the doctor. I'll tell you who it was. It was Jack Halloran. Jack helped."

"How did you get the mattress out to the vacant lot that the women were laying on when you shot them?"

"I never shot no woman on a mattress!"

"Oh, yea, Ruthie, you shot women on the mattress. Because we found a mattress out on a vacant lot where you set it afire. And it hadn't burned up. And that was where the two women were laying side by each on this mattress. Because the blood spots were in two different spots on the mattress. And now, matter of fact, these women were sound asleep when you shot them weren't they?"

"No, no, they were fighting me."

"Ruthie, they wasn't fighting you. How could they be fighting you when you had them both in the bed there and you shot them straight down through the bed because the gunshots went through the mattress? How do you account for that Ruthie?"

Ruthie sat and stared at the ground. "Well, Jack Halloran helped me do it. And he said I should do that in order to get rid of the bodies."

"I said a while ago you told us that a doctor did that. Now Ruthie your story is all wet," Arnold shifted forward in his seat, narrowing his eyes. "Let me tell you the story. You went out there with this gun to kill these women because this one woman had rejected your love isn't that right? You found them sound asleep and you had the key to the door so you went quietly in there to where they were sleeping and you shot them right through the bed there. Because on this mattress that you drug out to the vacant lot and tried to burn there's two spots of blood not one, not a big spot, not a little spot but two spots in the mattress where the hole went through. Ain't that right, Ruthie?"

Tears began to well in Ruth's eyes. She gulped hard.

"Then you cut them up back there in the bath tub, you want to make this story good about fighting so I said you shot yourself through the hand, didn't you?"

"No, no, no, I never had any gun."

"Oh yes, Ruthie, you had a gun. A little automatic. Same gun you shot the women with. I found the bullet under bathtub that you shot yourself through the hand with."

Ruth broke down and began to cry. "I'm not telling you anything. I'm not saying anything. I'm not talking to you again, ever!"

Upon her arrest, Ruth became the O.J. Simpson of her day. The people of the 1930s were unused to the immorality depicted in Judd's crime-murder, infidelity, lesbianism, and drug use. They was conjecture that Agnes "Anne" and Hedvig "Sammy" Samuelson were "lesbian party girls" who seduced Ruth into their lifestyle of debauchery and perversion along with their mutual boyfriend, Jack Halloran.

CHAPTER FOUR – SELF DEFENSE OR PRE-MEDIATION?

Ruth would describe her murders of Annie and Sammy as incidents of self-defense. She described getting into an altercation with Sammy initially, describing how Sammy took out a gun and threatened to blow her brains out. Ruth said that she fought back and they both struggled with the gun.

"I went into the kitchen to set down some tapioca dessert," Winnie recalled. "We were all in our pajamas. I went to put this down on the sink and Sammy came at me with a gun. She came through the breakfast room door."

"We quarreled violently," Winnie said. "About what I was going to tell about them and what they were going to tell my husband about me and so forth. That I had gone out with Jack. So the fact that it took place in the breakfast room door. I'm naturally left handed. I do many things with my left hand. I grabbed the gun with this hand (her left) and the shot went through there (her palm.)And I grabbed a bread knife on the table and I stabbed her twice in the (left) shoulder. And the knife bent, it was a bread knife, so I grabbed her hand like this (pulling her wrist back) and we both had our hands on the gun and one shot went through one of her fingers. I don't know which one. And one went through her chest. And one bullet jammed and caught me here (her left ring finger), at the top of the gun. And Ann came from behind. She got the ironing board from behind the water heater and came up behind me and hit me which caused us both to fall in the doorway. And we fought back and forth, wrestling for the gun in the door way, both of us on the floor. And the blood was all underneath the linoleum that was the only way it got there it was from the fight. She was not shot in bed like they say! It was in the doorway and the kitchen. It wasn't in the bedroom at all."

Ruth then called Jack to help dispose of the dead bodies.

"Jack cut up Sammy's body," Ruth said initially. "I couldn't do it."

She would later recant on that claim and state that Jack Halloran had called up a "Dr. Brown" and had him come over to cut up the bodies. She said that Halloran had some "dirt" on the doctor which coerced the physician to come over to the home and become complicit in the murder.

"Jack came with me," Ruth said. "And he picked Sammy up and carried her in (to the bed). And he got Doctor Brown. They took me home because I was hysterical."

Ruth would also claim later that she had gone to Anne and Sammy's home for a game of bridge. A fourth woman was there but had left. She testified that there was an argument about Halloran's introduction to another woman and that Annie and Sammy attacked her.

Ruth stated that Halloran came to the bungalow and after seeing the bodies, began plotting a way to "fix things". He went to the garage and came back with a "great, heavy trunk".

"Don't say a word to anyone," he warned her.

Halloran would be blamed for being an accomplice in the crime but after further research the decision not to prosecute him seemed to be the right one, particularly with the half-baked imagination of Ruth.

Her stories would remain inconsistent during her interrogation with Detective Arnold as well.

"So we interviewed her for about an hour," Arnold recalled. "And she'd tell us one story and we'd head her off on that. And then she'd sit there for a few minutes and she'd say well, 'That's right, but I'm gonna tell you the truth now!' And she'd tell us another story. We asked her 'where's the knife that you used to cut these women up with?' 'I never cut no women up!' 'Oh yes, yes you must have because there were in your trunk. Where's the knife?' 'I never had any knife.' 'Well who cut the women up?' 'Well, the doctor cut 'em up.' 'A doctor helped you cut them up?' 'No, a doctor cut them up. He was there. He's my friend.'

It was discovered during the investigation that Jack Halloran and Ruth were having an affair. Halloran himself became under suspicion for the killings and was indicted by a grand jury on December 30th, 1932.

Ruth would become the primary witness through a preliminary hearing which lasted three days.

"I am going to be hanged for something Jack Halloran is responsible for," Winnie said. *"I was convicted of murder, but I shot in self-defense[1]. Jack Halloran removed every bit of evidence. He is responsible for me going through all this. He is guilty of anything I am guilty of."*

Even Dr. Judd, the husband of Ruth, believed that the man with whom is wife cheated with was not capable of the crime.

"I know Jack Halloran," Dr. Judd said. "And it is very difficult for me to believe that Jack had anything to do with that."

Halloran did not bother to take the stand during his hearing. His attorney informed the court that Ruth's stories were the rantings of a crazy woman. He argued further that since Winnie claimed that she

---

1. *https://en.wikipedia.org/wiki/Self-defense*

killed the two women in self-defense there was no crime committed and Halloran was guilty of nothing.

The judge agreed, freeing Halloran in the belief that putting him to trial would be "an idle gesture."

"Jack Halloran had no more to do with the case than I did," Detective Arnold said. "She tried to involve Jack Halloran to get him to finance her defense. And when she fell down on it well, naturally she told a story that Jack helped her cut up the bodies and so on. But she already told that a doctor that helped her but she never would give us the doctor's name."

The controversy surrounding the case did irreparable damage to Halloran's reputation. He would lose valuable business contacts and his social standing in the community. Six years later, he would die at suddenly at the age of fifty-two.

CHAPTER FIVE – A LETTER OF CONFESSION

In 1931, Ruth would write out her "true confession" letter below and deliver it to her attorney. This letter detailed both the events of the night of the murder and her thought processes. Her attorney, Howard Richardson, did not use the letter. He instead had it "buried" as he tried to get her off on an insanity plea.

"I am writing the absolute truth of this case, in full confidence, that you will use it as you see fit in your best judgment. Mr. Richardson, I have full confidence in you and trust you.

This is my first and only confession of the case of the homicide of Anne LeRoi and Hedvig Samuelson. Anne was used to the world, I truly was not. Jack was the only man I had gone with since my marriage. I was ashamed of things I had done. I could not openly compete with her, I was married and ashamed to. Day after day she lorded it over me, always smiling and fresh and sweet, well knowing she was hurting me with her taunts. Many evenings Anne would kiss Jack and caress him in our presence, then after he was gone gloat over not caring a thing for him but merely working him for money. It was not what Jack did but the continual taunts made by Anne which drove me beside myself . . . I could not stand taunts. I just went crazy. Those taunts kept me awake, I could not sleep. I cried. I even prayed. I wrote my parents to please come to me. I was losing my mind. Wild ideas kept me awake. I took sleeping sedatives, Luminal. I wrote Doctor my nerves were breaking. I couldn't eat. I couldn't sleep. I loved Anne still, but those taunts. I would take more medicine to quiet my nerves, cried to please get things off my mind, to sleep. Friday night I expected Jack. He did not come. I went to bed. Again I could not sleep. I got up, went over to Anne's house. My brain whirling. I was so excited I was panting for breath. Never did I have the slightest dream of hurting Sammy. She simply never entered my mind. Except to get Anne, stop those taunts so I could sleep. Nothing more did I think of. I took the gun and a knife. How I would do it I was not sure. But I had no intention of harming Sammy. Jack was as intimate with Sammy as Anne, but it was Anne's cruel taunts that haunted me. . . . I hid in the house next door. Anne and Sammy returned to the bedroom . . . After they retired, I went to the back door, laid the knife and my shoes outside the door, then crept in the unlocked front door . . . I sat down on the couch in the same dark room and soon fell to sleep clutching the gun. I awakened, Sammy had gone to the bathroom, that insane desire, that power lead me on, I started for Anne. My stomach was turning inside out really twitching, jumping out of me, outside not a tremor, but my stomach jumping like convulsions. I retreated, curled up and went to sleep again. I went back to sleep again. Oh again and again all night I don't know how many times. Sammy kept going to the bathroom, I started for that bedroom and retreated each time so exhausted I immediately went to sleep.

Morning! I heard the milk man. Sammy went to the bathroom again. I started to call her, tell her I was there. I really did. Then I began shaking inside and remembered what I had come to do so this time I crept past the bathroom door, shot Anne. It was a low shot. Sammy called, What fell, Anne? I was hurrying past the door Sammy came out demanded to know what was the matter. I was limp she completely took the gun from my hands. I was non-resistant. I said, Sammy, I am crazy. I have lost my mind give me that gun and I will blow my brains out right here in this door. She held the gun and said, you get out of here right this minute.

... I then picked up the knife and went back after her with the knife. As I grabbed for the gun, I stabbed her in the shoulder, the fight with Sammy in that breakfast room door; her own finger on the trigger when the shot went through her chest; our fight is all about as I have always related she shot me through the hand as I grabbed for the gun; the gun jammed; we fell to the floor, struggled and I finally got the gun and shot her and in my wild state I really do not remember where in the head. I pulled Sammy into the bathroom. I cleaned up the floor I pulled in the trunk from the garage. It was now about 6:30 or 7 a.m. . . . I tugged and pulled and finally got Anne from the bed into the trunk. Now it doesn't sound possible but this all took about two hours. I left for the office . . . I had pulled the trunk with Anne's body into the living room. But the trunk was unlocked. Sammy was on the bathroom floor all day Saturday . . . This all happened in the morning. I stayed in my office . . . until 4 p.m. I then took the bag home with me with the gun, knife, pajamas and dress. I fed my cat and went back to the 2929 N. 2nd Street house at around 6 p.m. I really had nothing definite in my mind. No plans made. In fact except for an irresistible impulse to get Anne I had no other plans. I entered the house through the bathroom window getting a chair from next door to climb in. I pulled the trunk back into the hall tried to lift Sammy into it, but that was utterly impossible, I couldn't possibly lift her, she was too heavy her body was stiff. I then got two cheap knives from the kitchen and severed her body into portions I could lift. I was hours doing this and then inch by inch pulling the trunk back into the living room."

CHAPTER SIX – THE TRIAL

Three months after the bodies had been discovered, Judd's trial began. Ruth would not be tried for the murder of Sammy, only the murder of Agnes.

Richardson would be steadfast in his defense that Ruth was innocent by reason of insanity. He didn't allow her to take the stand. He kept the existence of Ruth's confessional letter to himself.

The case went to trial with the prosecutors taking aim at Ruth's self-defense alibi. They pointed out the fact that Ruth did not have a bullet wound in her hand when she showed up for work the day after and that her wound was, in fact, self-inflicted to confuse authorities. They further argued that Ruth killed the two women out of a jealous rage as she did not want her husband to find out about her affair with Jack Halloran.

The jurors agreed with the prosecution and found Ruth guilty of two counts of first-degree murder.

She was sentenced to death by hanging.

Ruth then behaved oddly in jail, screaming, yelling and making bizarre gestures. Because of her high-profile case, the Arizona governor gave her a special sanity hearing that took place only three days before her scheduled death-by-hanging.

This hearing became a spectacle for the media. Ruth put on a show, laughing inappropriately, clapping her hands, screaming obscenities at the jury and pulling out clumps of her hair. She then tried to take off her clothes and had to be restrained.

"She's been crazy all her life," Ruth's mother would testify during the hearing. "More or less."

"She comes from a long, lineage of crazy folk," Winnie's father, the Methodist preacher revealed. "Our family has been cursed with madness for over 125 years. It goes all the way back to Scotland."

The testimony worked and Ruth's death sentence was commuted to a life prison term. She was then sent to an Arizona state hospital for the criminally insane.

CHAPTER SEVEN – FUGITIVE ON THE RUN

Ruth would show a dramatic improvement in her mental stability during her stay at the hospital. She no longer displayed the same screaming fits or displays of anger. She fit in with the prison population and embrace the routine, all the while calculating ways to escape.

She left behind a "dummy" in her bed, made up of items around the sanitarium. Fooling the guards, she slipped out of the mental hospital only to be recaptured days later.

The prison guards had her on close watch upon her return but Ruth was determined.

She would escape a total of seven times. On one occasion, Ruth walked all the way from Phoenix to Yuma, Arizona, making her way along the Southern Pacific railroad tracks. These escapes would become a national joke because on slow news days reporters would remark, "maybe Winnie Ruth Judd will escape again."

These escapes would become a running gag among the more sensationalist newspapers. One magazine opened an article on Judd with the words : "When you read this story, the country's cleverest maniac may be at large again, perhaps walking down your street, or sitting next to you."

Ruth would return to her sanitarium after another escape in 1952. Inexplicably, she would be called to testify before a grand jury that was investigating state hospital conditions.

Ever the opportunist, Ruth would plot out another escape during her transport to the hearing. She was searched beforehand, however, and prison guards found a key hidden in her hair and a razor blade concealed beneath her tongue.

A year later, Ruth would have another sanity hearing. During this time she would spent a great deal of time trying to obtain her letter of confession back from her attorney Howard Robinson's widow to get this letter back. She had enough wherewithal to realize that if the letter would be made public it would be incriminating evidence against her insanity defense.

Richardson's widow did not comply but the letter would not be revealed until after Ruth's death.

CHAPTER EIGHT – THE GREAT ESCAPE

Ruth would stage her most successful escape on October 8th, 1963.

She coerced a friend to give her the key to the front door of the hospital and made her way out undetected in the middle of the night.

"About these seven escapes," Arnold said. "The woman, in my opinion, its just my opinion, but I've been around. This woman never escaped out there. She was turned loose every time she went away from that asylum. They wanted to get rid of her! And she wasn't getting seen very fast according to their opinion. And every time she went out of there she'd go out and try to get money from some of her old friends to leave town on and she couldn't get the money. Then somebody would see her and turn her in and then of course the hospital would have to go back and get her. And put her back in the hospital. And that was carried on there for a number of years as I say as everybody knows she's supposedly escaped from there seven times. Before she got enough money to leave town on (laughs)."

Ruth somehow made her way from the Arizona sanitariums to the San Francisco Bay Area where she took on the name of "Marian Lane."

She lived with the wealthy Nichols family, finding work as their live-in maid.

"One of the reasons I came here (to San Francisco) was to be near him (her husband)," Winnie said. "He's buried here in the Golden Gate National Military Cemetery. And when I go down there frequently, I put violets on his grave. I thought he was a wonderful person. He was ill and he was worth saving. And I worked very hard. Ms. Nickles knew I loved violets so she had a whole lot planted so I could pick them anytime and take them to his grave. Because I was buying violets and she said I'll plant the violets, she was that kind and good to me."

Her identity was eventually discovered and she was recaptured after six years of freedom. Ruth would hire attorney Melvin Belli to represent her and he fought her extradition to Arizona. Governor

Ronald Reagan, however, personally intervened, sending Ruth back to Arizona.

Ruth would be tried again and judged sane, thus ending her stays at sanitariums. She was sent to jail but only incarcerated for an additional two years.

Ruth would be paroled on December 22nd, 1971. Upon her release she moved to Stockton, California where she lived out the rest of her life without incident. In 1983, the state of Arizona gave her an "absolute discharge" which meant that she was no longer a parolee of the state.

Winnie Ruth Judd would die on October 23rd, 1998 at the age of ninety-three.

CHURCH LADY AND KILLER: THE TRUE STORY OF BLANCHE MOORE

KATIE WALLS

"People couldn't believe that she did what she did. People became fascinated that how could someone who on the surface could be so nice, could be capable of such a heinous crime." - Paula Orange

Blanche Taylor Moore was born on February 17th, 1933 in North Carolina, the fifth of seven children. Her father was Parker Davis Kiser, a self-taught minister who had both a drinking and gambling problem. Her mother, Flonnie Honeycutt, held little sway in the goings on in the Kiser household. Flonnie would work in the local mills, bringing home $40 a week. She turned the money over to her husband who promptly turned around and spent the money on younger women. When he wasn't chasing young tail, Kiser did various odd jobs to support the family, primarily working in a sawmill then later as an insurance salesman. His primary occupation, however, was the seduction of women that he came across in both bars and churches.

Despite his roving eye, the Reverend Kiser was a strict father who didn't allow any of his children to participate in school activities or spend hanging out with friends.

Living a double life, P.D. Kiser's gambling debts increased to the point where he made the decision to sell young Blanche off as a prostitute to pay off his debts which he incurred during card games.

After one losing streak, Reverend Kiser took his adolescent daughter for a drive and pulled over to the side of the road.

"I'm going to pull up under that tree," Kiser said. "When I do, I want you to go fuck that man."

"P.D. Kiser was an alcoholic and self-righteous country minister," said psychologist Grant Kelleher. "Despite efforts to abstain from alcohol he always relapsed. Blanche's childhood was utterly destroyed by her father and she lived in a childhood prison of despair."

Blanche, desperate to leave the abusive household, married James Taylor in May of 1952. Blanche was nineteen years old at the time, Taylor was twenty-four. She would give birth to their first daughter, Vanessa, in 1953.

Blanche was the typical Southern diva, confident in her ability to seduce any man she wanted but found the pickings slim in her small North Carolina town. She was attractive by most accounts, having long black hair and eyes that "were so dark they looked black."

"Blanche's face was sculpted in the high bird-boned features of the very prettiest Appalachian women," one researcher said. "Long, lithe, with generous breasts and a sleek round bottom perched on slender, perfectly shaped legs."

"She flew her small burgh of Tarheel by grabbing the first man who asked her to marry him. Young Blanche was left with one overwhelming wish for the future-to leave her perverse, sermonizing father and begin a new life that was far away from his abuse."

Finances were tough and Blanche was forced to work as a cashier at the Kroger supermarket. She would toil on the job for six years before giving birth to her second child, Cindi, in 1953. Still, she became a popular fixture at the market as folks would line up at her register just to have a quick chat with the friendly Blanche. She would remain a mainstay at the supermarket for decades.

"She was always friendly to customers and her co-workers," a former Kroger employee said. "You would have never guessed her as being unhappy or mean to anyone. Just wasn't in her."

Her tenure at Kroger's looked to be mixed, however, as Blanche could be moody. But the management hierarchy gave her high marks in her job performance and labeled her as a "good leader" as she trained other grocery checkers.

Still, a dark side emerged.

"She could be vindictive," said one co-worker who asked not to be identified. "If you got on her bad side, watch out. She was two-faced. Two-faced and underhanded. There was one incident where a large bag of cash wound up missing.

Management would have to explain why her store was the only store that didn't turn a profit."

BAD MARRIAGE

By 1959, things had soured at the home front. Blanche and James had several loud fights in public. Blanche was dragged behind a car on one occasion and in another, she was confronted about an affair with a customer at the Kroger supermarket.

Despite her peculiar manner, Blanche would be promoted to "head cashier" which was the equivalent of a store manager in today's corporate climate. This was one of the few top positions open to Kroger's women employees at that time. She would also sell Tupperware at home parties which she used as a cover to seduce different men that interested her.

Her husband James seemed powerless against the woman he married. He worked as a furniture restorer but jobs were few and far between for the former military veteran who had just returned from the Korean War. James was described as a "burly man" that was "quick to anger." He spent the majority of his time editing sermons taken from the Glen Hope Baptist church and sending them overseas for missionaries to spread the gospel. He also began drowning himself in alcohol which was much to Blanche's disappointment.

"Blanche had, in essence, married a carbon copy of her father," forensic psychologist Paula Orange said. "James was like her dad in that he was a compulsive gambler and was horrible with money. He would disappear on the weekend and come back flat broke."

Her own father wouldn't behave much better, leaving Blanche's mother in 1960 as he vowed to "find himself a younger woman."

Blanche then acted out on her own. She continued to use the supermarket as her own personal singles bar, having affairs with numerous customers and male supervisors.

James would find out about her affairs and would threaten to leave Blanche. The two would continue to have violent, explosive arguments but ultimately James would never follow through on his threats to leave.

A NEW MAN

By 1962, however, Blanche would have her sights set on a new assistant manager by the name of Raymond Reid.

Reid was already married with two young children and initially spurned the advances of the slightly older Blanche.

But what Blanche wanted, Blanche got. It took three years of flirting to finally get Raymond to lower his guard. Blanche seduced the married man but continued to sleep with other male companions she met through the store.

To further complicate her life, Blanche's father had taken ill shortly after she arrived to make some sort of attempt at reconciliation.

Blanche remained at his bedside and helped to try and nurse him back to health. The elder Kiser, however, was too far gone. He died due to "heart attack triggered by chronic emphysema."

Doctors completely overlooked the fact that Kiser had suffered from violent stomach cramps, diarrhea, vomiting, delirium and a blue skin pallor.

This all pointed to death by arsenic poisoning but they had no reason to suspect Blanche of anything.

Noting the ease with she got away with her father's death, Blanche set her sights on the other man who was an obstacle to her happiness.

Her husband, James Taylor would suffer a near-fatal heart attack. His brush with death forced him to "get right with God" and he attempted to reconcile with Blanche.

"James Taylor's life trajectory was strikingly similar to that of Blanche's father, Parker Davis," Orange said. "Like Davis, he would find religion later in life and put on the pretense of a changed man. Blanche saw through it all, she herself was used to men using religion as a prop much like her father. But she put up appearances for appearance sake."

Blanche would later describe James as becoming "the perfect husband and father" but her six-year affair with Raymond Reid continued.

Despite their marital infidelity, Blanche would try and persuade Reid to attend church with her.

"I have been quite religious all my life, or I was," Blanche recalled. "I was very active in the First Disciples until the fire. After that, I just lost my interest in religion."

With his wife deeply entrenched in an affair, James would come down with the "flu" in September of 1970. He started to lose his hair, had diarrhea, swollen glands, blood stool and blue skin pallor. All the signs of arsenic poisoning yet no one who examined him was any the wiser. He would be hospitalized at the end of the month and die a few dies after his admission, shortly after Blanche brought him some ice cream.

Blanche would then help take care of James' mother, Isla, up until her death on November 25th, 1970. Doctors signed off on Isla's death as something attributed to natural causes. Inexplicably, they ignored the blue skin pallor on the woman as well as the undigested arsenic that remained in the Blanche's mother-in-law's stomach.

So within two months, Blanche had eliminated both her husband James and her mother-in-law, Isla. She was able to obtain a small portion of their estate and used the money to buy a home in Burlington, North Carolina.

Despite proceeds from these deaths, her co-workers thought she may have been "tapping the till" at work as there was no way she could afford such a home on the meager inheritance.

COAST IS CLEAR

Raymond Reid would decide to go all in on his affair with Blanche. He left his wife and children in 1971, a full nine years after first meeting Blanche. He got himself a small apartment and filed for divorce from his wife, fully expecting Blanche to become his bride.

Blanche would stop by at Reid's new place, cook him breakfast and sexually entertain him. She said that Reid was "helpless" without her.

This caused a stir not only in their workplace but in the small town in which they both lived.

"Mom never expected to spend the rest of her life by herself. She had too much to offer," said Blanche's daughter Cynthia Chatman.

"Reid was a very good man. He was good to us," said Vanessa, Blanche's other daughter.

Blanche herself didn't feel that way. As a future district attorney said while investigating Blanche's story, she would soon deem the young Reid as someone who "wasn't good enough, she wanted to date someone better. She was very blunt about that."

Blanche had a foul mouth and often said things that were inappropriate. Once she told the friend of her son-in-law, "you know what you really need? You need a really good blow job. If I went down on you, it'd probably kill you. You probably couldn't handle it."

She wouldn't limit her romantic encounters with the male supervisors like Reid at the supermarket. She targeted anyone she found handsome as when a new delivery man entered the store, Blanche said, "Man, I'd like to see the dick on that guy."

SEXUAL HARASSMENT

The highly sexual Blanche would claim sexual harassment during her tenure at Kroger's. A top company official named Robert J. Hutton paid a visit to her store. Blanche would contend that he made advances and fondled female cashiers.

"He reached him up my dress, exposed himself and grabbed my buttocks," Blanche said as she recalled an encounter with Hutton. "He had his pants down and asked 'Are you ready for this?'"

Blanche then picked up Hutton's pants and underwear as she fled from the store. EmbaRrassed, Hutton had to borrow a meat cutter's smock before exiting the store.

Blanche didn't return to Kroger's after the incident. She filed a sexual harassment suit and began seeing psychiatrists. One of her doctors, Dr. Jesse N. McNeil said in an affidavit that Blanche suffered from "depression, anxiety, and a serious suicidal condition. She felt completely alienated and antagonistic toward men and has not been able to maintain any meaningful social contacts with members of the opposite sex.

Her defense attorney would later dismiss the affidavit as "hyperbole" to bolster the charges of the sexual harassment suit.

It would later be revealed that Blanche had a flirtatious relationship with Hutton before she filed suit. She was on the lookout for someone "better" than Reid and thought that Hutton may fit the bill. But the relationship soured and Hutton ultimately lost his job.

Kroger would settle out of court with Blanche, paying the flirtatious young cashier a lump-sum payment of $275,000.

YET ANOTHER RUSE

Always on the lookout for "quick cash," Blanche concocted a scheme to collect some fire insurance in 1985. A mysterious fire broke out at her home and Blanche put the blame on a local "pervert", a man that she claimed to have seen lurking around her property.

"I saw a man," Blanche said. "He was creeping around the side wall."

"Did you call the cops?"

"No," Blanche said. "He was, you know, touching himself. Touching himself down there. I screamed and he ran away."

Firefighters agreed that arson was the cause and did not question her tale of the unknown "pervert" who set her home ablaze. Blanche would take the proceeds from the fire insurance and purchase a mobile home.

A month later, however, the mobile home was burned to the ground. Blanche once again blamed a "pervert" whom she said followed her to the trailer home. The authorities believed her and she collected another fire insurance check.

"Really not sure what Blanche was doing with all this money," Orange said. "She had to have over a quarter of a million dollars on hand from inheritances and sexual harassment suits. She soon realized that money could be gained quicker through settlements as opposed to hard work."

Still on the lookout for a "new man," Blanche met the acquaintance of the Reverend Dwight Moore on Easter Sunday of 1985.

Moore was the pastor of the Carolina United Church of Christ. Divorced with two grown children of his own, the fifty-one-year-old preacher immediately caught the eye of the forty-two-year-old Blanche.

She introduced herself at the end of his sermon and complimented him on his speaking ability. He soon began "counseling" her as her impending lawsuit with Kroger came to a head.

The two got to know each other and Blanche was judgmental toward the Reverend when she found out that his own marriage ended when he was discovered to have an affair with another woman in his church. But Moore was taken by the beauty and Southern charm of Blanche and would not be denied.

"Moore saw Blanche as the innocent victim," Orange said. "She could do no wrong in his eyes and this blinded him to a lot of things, mainly the fact that she had instigated the flirtation and was still involved with Reid. And oh yeah, she just killed her husband. But Blanche saw opportunity in the Reverend. The preacher man was divorced and the pastor of a relatively small church. So she probably saw authority in that. She liked men in the authority, whether it be a manager at Kroger's or a man giving a sermon in a small church."

It began platonic enough, at first, the two began meeting for lunch then dinner on a "friends" basis. Blanche did begin dropping hints that they shouldn't be surprised if she married a "preacher man" in the near future.

"The Reverend was putty in the hands of a seductress like Blanche," Orange said. "Blanche could quote scripture then talk explicitly about sex. She put up a false front of a churchgoing woman but had a carnal way about her. The Reverend took one look at her and thought to himself 'we got a live one here!'"

Moore was smitten and his phone calls to Blanche increased over time. He would leave notes on Blanche's front doorstep which were sometimes intercepted by Blanche's daughters.

The Reverend would invite Blanche out to "get some ice cream" and the two would soon arrive together as church gatherings.

"She was dating both the Reverend Moore and Raymond Reid," Orange said. "Her daughters believed that her relationship with Reid had cooled off but nobody told Raymond. Moore seemed none the wiser that Blanche was still seeing Reid. So Blanche was playing both sides against the other. If things worked out with the Reverend she would dump Reid."

Reid would not go away easy. He had abandoned his own wife over twelve years earlier in the hopes of eventually marrying Blanche.

"She couldn't just break-up with Reid," Orange said. "She was in too deep. She got to know his family and friends. The expectation was that they were going to get married but for whatever reason in Blanche's mind, she held out. So, rather than string him along further she decided to eliminate him from the equation."

Reid came down with a case of the "shingles" in 1986 as he developed a skin condition that would point to arsenical peripheral neuritis.

By April, he would be hospitalized with the same symptoms as Blanche's previous victims. This would include diarrhea, projectile vomiting and a loss of sensation in both his hands and feet.

Again, physicians dropped the ball in assessing these classic warning signs of arsenic poisoning. The doctors ordered special tests for "heavy metals intoxication" as well as a urine test which showed six times the normal amount of arsenic in Reid's system.

The report never reached the desk of the doctor's and Reid would continue to suffer.

Blanche would play the role of the dutiful girlfriend but again her inappropriate comments would be put on display when on occasion Reid's son Steve left the room with an attractive young woman. When the young man returned, Blanche asked: "Well, did you fuck her?"

The young man looked on in shock then denied the accusation.

"Well, why not? Growing boy your age needs some pussy once in a while. What's the last time you had some good pussy?"

DEVOTED GIRLFRIEND

When she wasn't harassing Reid's young son, Blanche would be by the side of the sick man on a daily basis. She put on a false front to Reid and his nurses, quoting the Bible and giving the impression that she was a compassionate, Christian woman attending to the needs of her boyfriend.

"She made quite an impression on the nurses on duty," Orange said. "They would testify later that she was the epitome of the caring girlfriend. She showed the man compassion and caring and they all thought that he was very lucky to have Blanche Taylor Moore in his life."

Reid would be diagnosed with Guillain-Barre Syndrome, an auto-immune disorder with the symptoms being muscle weakness, nerve-tingling, and progressive fatigue.

"Raymond would die and be revived again," Orange said. "His heart failed and he would be declared clinically dead, losing heartbeat and respiration but the medical staff was able to revive him."

Blanche, however, would be waiting to provide "care" after the staff saved her boyfriend's life. She would come with a cup of processed food and eagerly feed Reed after his latest return from the dead. She would make a show of giving Reid her homemade pudding and specially made "milkshakes".

"Her demeanor was so sweet and unassuming that the nurses wouldn't even think of questioning her," Orange said. "They would nurse Reid back to health, get some of that poison out of his system then Blanche would come into the room with her 'concoctions.' It was literally one step forward and ten steps back for the poor man."

Raymond would recuperate then relapse again into respiratory arrest.

"Think of the worst flu you've ever had then multiply it by ten," Orange said. "Then you're resuscitated again and again. He was on a roller coaster for his life. Absolutely horrific. All the while, Blanche would witness Reid's battles with death. She knew she was the cause of it, with her arsenic milkshakes and pudding, yet she would stand there aghast, praying to the God above that Reid be delivered from the illness."

Reid would regain consciousness but remain confused. He would then began to recuperate and get his senses back. He would feel optimistic about his chances then he would relapse again.

Physical and psychological torture on repeat play.

This would continue for three months. Blanche seized the opportunity to have Reid create a living will. She named herself as executor and beneficiary to one-third of Reid's estate. The other two-thirds would be divided among his sons.

"Blanche had a way about her," Orange said. "She could talk just about any man into doing anything for her. A great deal of her ability to have gotten away with the things she did was her own persona. By this time, she had killed her father, first husband, and her mother-in-law with the exact same methods. Yet no one ever suspected anything or put two and two together, not even those closest to her. Her persona was so ingratiating and unassuming that it would be unthinkable."

After the will was drawn out, Reid's health rapidly deteriorated. In October of 1986, he was brought into intensive care suffering from renal and respiratory failure. He would die three days later as his body began bloating so severely that his skin ripped apart.

According to her daughters, Blanche seemed torn up that Reid had passed away.

Doctor's blamed Guillain-Barre syndrome but wanted an autopsy to be certain. Blanche declined, manipulating Reid's sons into agreeing with her that no autopsy be performed.

"Blanche was like most serial killers," Orange said. "Narcissistic. She thought she was special. She thought she was smarter than everyone else and that she would never be caught."

This now opened the door to a relationship with the Reverend Moore.

"The coast was clear," Orange said.

The Reverend accompanied Blanche to Reid's funeral. She had acquired over $30,000 from Redis's estate in addition to pilfering his safe deposit box and the safe in his home. Reid's sons also gave Blanche over $45,000 from their father's life insurance in the belief that "he would have wanted it that way."

"Then the Reverend didn't waste any time," Orange said. "After an obligatory period of grieving, the Reverend pursued her with great fervor until she finally relented and the two had a wedding date set for August of 1987, less than ten months after Reid's death. Blanche now had a sizable nest egg but most likely lost it all through audacious spending and mismanagement. She had money acquired from the sexual harassment suit, her first husband, and now money gained through her manipulation of Reid's will. She got addicted to the scheming. The game playing and manipulation. It was all an adrenaline rush to her."

THE PERFECT WOMAN

To Moore's family and friends, Blanche seemed like the perfect woman for him. She put on a front of knowing the Bible backward and forwards, having the personality of a "church lady" to match.

"Behind the scenes," Orange said. "Both the Reverend and Blanche knew better. She was a hot number to be sure and everything that was repressed in the Reverend now came to fore. He would now have his cake and eat it too, the Southern man's dream of having a woman who is a lady in church but a tiger in bed."

Things were looking rosy until Blanche was diagnosed with breast cancer. She had one breast surgically removed in order to stop the spread. She went into recovery and the couple pushed the marriage ceremony back another year, to November 27th, 1988.

Things were still not meant to be, however, as three weeks before the wedding the Reverend Moore came down with a mysterious illness all his own. He suffered from vomiting and diarrhea so severe that he had to be hospitalized. Doctors would discover an "intestinal blockage" in the preacher and he was forced to undergo surgery.

Blanche and the Reverend were finally able to tie the knot in April of 1989.

The wedding was simple and witnessed by only two church members.

"She had on a real pretty dress," Doris Pender said, one of the witnesses. "They were beaming. It seemed like there was electricity there. It seemed like they were very much in love."The two lovebirds would go to Montclair, New Jersey for their honeymoon and also visit the Reverend Moore's first grandchild who had just been born.

The honeymoon would be short-lived as the Reverend Moore collapsed on a homeward bound trip five days later.

"There are two competing stories," Orange said. "One is that he ate a pastry then collapsed. The other is that he was spraying insect repellent on some flowers outside his home. Blanche came back with a chicken sandwich for him which promptly made the Reverend sick."

The symptoms eventually grew worse and the Reverend insisted on going to the hospital. He was admitted to the Alamance County Hospital on April 28th and his condition worsened after Blanche delivered some "homemade soup."

The doctors inexplicably sent him home but Moore's condition would worsen after he consumed another one of Blanche's meals. She would then drive him to North

Carolina Memorial hospital which refused admittance without a written order from Alamance County.

The Reverend had now retained forty pounds of body fluid while Blanche got the necessary paperwork. She would then relay to the Reverend's family that he "was fine, we're just going to do some tests."

Moore's symptoms mirrored that of Guillain-Barre syndrome, the medical staff became suspicious because of the speed of which the symptoms appeared.

"This go around the medical staff tested him for arsenic poisoning," Orange said. "They found huge doses of the poison in his system and immediately suspected that Blanche had given it to him."

The Reverend fought back successfully against the poison. He was able to recuperate and was released from the hospital.

"Reverend Moore set a medical record," Orange said. "The physicians on duty noted that he had survived a dosage of arsenic higher than anyone on record. There was enough poison to kill a moose. Yet the Reverend survived. Amazing."

The police were summoned and became suspicious when they began investigating the number of people associated with Blanche that had died under similar circumstances.

"She didn't do anything," the Reverend Moore said when asked by the police if he believed that Blanche was to blame for his illness. "No way. Not my Blanche. I think I must have inhaled poison while I was spraying the garden for pests."

But the police saw a pussy-whipped man when they saw one. They proceeded to question Blanche who would deny bringing any food to Raymond Reid while he was hospitalized. The claim was contradicted by hospital staffers who were on hand to witness Blanche force Reid to drink one of her "homemade milkshakes."

Investigating further, authorities found out that Blanche had tried to get the Reverend's pension revised so that she would be the principal beneficiary. Blanche became worried that they would test the Reverend for arsenic poison. She had her husband's hair shaved bald but investigating officials were able to obtain samples from the Reverend's pubic region and tested that.

"Both Dwight (Reverend Moore) and Raymond felt depressed," Blanche said when asked why both of her lovers tested high for arsenic. "They were probably taking arsenic themselves."

Police would charge Blanche with assault and had the body of Reid exhumed on his body, consistent with those found on the body of her first husband, James Taylor.

The chief medical examiner would discover that Reid's illness was not only the cause of arsenic but that he continued to receive the poison while he was in the hospital.

The Reverend would refuse to believe that his wife would do such a thing. It took six weeks but the police finally convinced him otherwise after they exhumed the bodies of Raymond Reid and James Taylor.

"You're lucky," the detective informed him. "Damn lucky you're even alive."

The Reverend then confronted Blanche about the accusations he heard from the police. He informed her that their marriage was over. The decision was an emotionally devastating one for the Reverend as Blanche left his hospital bedside covered in crocodile tears.

MOTIVATION?

The townsfolk and those close to Blanche immediately wanted to know why. Why would such a sweet and unassuming woman commit such diabolical crimes? The district attorney, however, couldn't care less. He just knew that the crimes had taken place.

"We don't have to get into why," the DA said. "When you start looking for a rational motive, you generally start overthinking. I just know that this guy died and the state medical examiner said he had a fatal level of arsenic in him."

Blanche was arrested and charged with the murder of Raymond Reid which the DA felt would be easier to prove than the Reverend's poisoning.

During the trial, which opened in Winston-Salem on October 21st, 1990, Blanche continued to deny giving Reid any food. The state produced over fifty-three witnesses who contradicted her statement. Reid's ex-wife and sons also sued Baptist Hospital for malpractice.

During her trial, jurors would discover how Blanche would kill her victims with kindness. She would place the arsenic in the food she would bring for him until ultimately he died.

"Raymond Reid lay in Baptist Hospital flat on his back, bed sores on his back, completely unable to move, tears in his eyes on the days that this woman who was killing him doesn't come," lead prosecutor Janet Branch told the jury, tears streaming down her face.

"He's crying because his murderer isn't coming to see him! Can you imagine anything more pitiful in this whole world? And he loves her with all his heart. ... But she's running around on him, and she's sleeping with Dwight Moore, and she's going to that hospital."

"I never felt the need for vengeance," Moore said. "I have no desire to see her executed. I don't even object to her efforts to get off death row. I have no feelings against her living out her final days in the most humane way possible."

"The authorities began to realize that they had a serial killer on their hands," Orange said. "They wanted to exhume the bodies of everyone that knew Blanche Taylor Moore in their lives. There was a bit of a hysteria going on. Ultimately, I think the authorities decided not to pursue the matter beyond what they could prove in court. The countless one night stands by Blanche would have been impossible to track considering her tenure at Kroger's."

They would exhume five bodies. Traces of arsenic were found in the bodies of both her first husband and her father.

She was cleared of any wrongdoing in her father's death but many believed that the trauma she suffered at the hands of her father led to her becoming a serial killer.

"Her father was a womanizer," Orange said. "And he had abandoned the family had some point. I think that perhaps she mirrored his behavior in her own life and took it a step further, taking out revenge on her father with the many men she came into contact with."

"It certainly isn't uncommon for female serial killers to carry bad relationships with their father into their future relationships with men."

"She is killing her father over and over again."

"I have no doubts as to her guilt," the Reverend Moore said. "The worst lingering effect has been tremors in my hands and weakness in my legs along with peripheral neuropathy. My feet and legs are pretty much a constant reminder (of Blanche).

Blanche Taylor Moore remains on death row in North Carolina. She is the oldest inmate on death row in the state.

OCCULT KILLER : THE TRUE STORY OF CLARA SCHWARTZ

AMY BRYANT

The story of Clara Schwartz is one of a troubled young woman who had a turbulent relationship with her father. While this is certainly not an unusual situation, the outcome, in the case, was deadly. In December of 2001, Schwartz enlisted the help of friends, including a mentally ill teenager, to murder her father Robert Schwartz. Through an elaborate and twisted role-playing game, Schwartz turned a few misfits into a band of loyal followers who would kill for her.

Schwartz had met Kyle Hulbert at a Renaissance fair in the fall of the same year. She told Hulbert horror stories about her father, claiming he abused her and that she feared he would soon try to poison her. Hulbert, who had a long history of mental illness, believed Schwartz without question. Schwartz invited Hulbert to take part in a role-playing game she had invented called Underworld.

Through this game, Schwartz used her character to convince Hulbert's character, an assassin, to kill her father. Sometime between when the game began and December of 2001, it became clear that Schwartz wanted her father dead in real life. Hulbert, all too willing to do whatever Schwartz said, agreed.

Hulbert, accompanied by two mutual friends of his and Schwartz's who were in on the game, drove to the country home of Robert Schwartz on December 8, 2001. He used a samurai sword to stab Robert over and over, leaving him for dead. It was only through the carelessness of Hulbert and his accomplices that the story of Schwartz and the deadly game she orchestrated came to light.

Early Life

Clara Schwartz was born in 1981 to Robert Schwartz and his wife. Clara was the youngest of the Schwartz's three children, which included herself, an older sister Catherine, and her older brother Jesse.

"Clara wasn't an attractive girl with lots of boyfriends," forensic psychologist Paula Orange said. "She had a hangdog look with a dull facial expression. Underneath her placid exterior was anger, however, an anger that was inexplicable given her privileged upbringing."

Robert Schwartz was a well-known researcher and scientist. He worked in the field of biometrics and DNA research, gaining national recognition for his work. Robert was also a founding member of the Virginia Biotechnology Association.

"Robert Schwartz was very respected in his field," Orange said. "He was responsible for some very advanced work in DNA mapping. He could solve almost any problem in the DNA field but could not solve the problems he had at home with his twenty-year old daughter."

Despite her father's successful career, Clara Schwartz was closer to her mother than her father. In fact, her relationship with her father Robert was strained for her whole life. The two argued frequently and never got along.

When Clara Schwartz was just a teenager, around the age of fifteen, her mother became sick with cancer and eventually passed away. After this tragedy, Clara withdrew even further from her father and her peers. She became a loner and dressed in the "goth" style, associating only with friends who were also part of the goth subculture.

"This would all look harmless at first glance," Orange said. "Clara was really into vampires and the subgenre of Goth music that catered to that crowd. She liked the role playing games but again, she was young and for most kids it is just a temporary escape from reality. The warning signs weren't really there other than the fact that she was cut from a different cloth than everyone else."

The role playing games, however, took a serious turn as Clara's hatred for her father grew.

"She played a role playing game called Quest V," Orange said. "I suppose you can describe it as an offshoot of Dungeons and Dragons. It was there hat she was able to escape from the dismal reality of not having her mother around anymore. That was the key word, escape. Here in the on-line world, she could be in conrol."

It was here that she would involve herself in an alternative circle of friends with unusual interests that ultimately helped Schwartz orchestrate her father's murder.

"Clara spent her days in her own little world," Orange said. "She would spend the entire day staring at her laptop with her earphones plugged in, typing away at her role playing games. She cared little for interpersonal interaction with other kids her age. Most all of her 'socializing', if you can call it that, took place in forums and game playing chat rooms."

The Crime

Previous Attempts

Clara Schwartz had been planning to kill her fifty-seven year old father for some time. During her murder trial, Schwartz's former boyfriend Patrick House testified about Schwartz's intentions dating back to before she had even met Kyle Hulbert, the man who would ultimately murder her father.

House stated that while he had been dating Schwartz, she often spoke about killing her father. She researched herbal poisons, saying that she wanted it to appear that her father died of natural causes. House also said that Schwartz discussed with him how much money she would inherit if her father were dead, and she was concerned that her father was going to cut her out of his will due to their rocky relationship.

"Clara always wanted to be in control," Orange said. "And I think she also saw dollar signs if her father died. She would have to split his fortune three-ways upon his death, so she would gain about four-hundred-thousand dollars."

Schwartz had also involved House in a roleplaying game she invented called Underworld. In this game, Clara called herself the "Lord of Chaos". House's character was an assassin. Schwartz began with roleplaying, asking House to kill her father in character. House, in his roleplaying character, agreed.

However, it progressed beyond simple roleplay. Schwartz began asking House when he was really going to kill her father. House became uneasy and ended things between the two of them.

Schwartz and Hulbert Meet

It was the fall of 2001 when Clara Schwartz and Kyle Hulbert met at a renaissance fair. Hulbert was a very troubled young man. Though he was only eighteen years old when he met Schwartz, Hulbert had already been placed in mental institutions seven different times in the past twelve years.

"Hulbert both looked and acted like a medical experiment gone bad," Orange said. "He had a large forehead and chin. He had shifty eyes that gave anyone who talked to him the impression that 'something is not right' about him."

Hulbert had several diagnoses of mental illness already as well. He suffered from both bipolar disorder and schizophrenia. Schizophrenia blurred the lines between fantasy and reality in Hulbert's mind, while bipolar disorder made him subject to fits of rage and aggressive behavior. Hulbert had just been released after his latest stay in a psychiatric facility four months before meeting Schwartz.

"Hulbert was a certifiable nut," Orange said. "Meeting Clara just sent him over the edge. He saw her as his queen and she saw him as a useful idiot. He showed up to the Renaissance fair wearing a cat mask while brandishing a two-foot sword. Anyone could see he was a nut. But Clara was intrigued."

Schwartz was nineteen years old and a student at James Madison University when she and Hulbert met. Though she was now in college, Schwartz and her father continued to have a rocky relationship. Schwartz was also heavily involved in goth subculture. She and Hulbert shared an interest in the occult, magic, and fantasy.

Schwartz introduced Hulbert to the roleplaying game she had invented called Underworld. Her friends Katherine Inglis and Michael Pfohl were also part of the game, acting as Schwartz's loyal followers.

"Inglis was bespectacled," Orange said. "She looked like the classic nerd, wide-eyed and naive. Pfohl had a creepy look about him, nerdy with glasses and a goatee. They were both not very bright and looked like people you would see in a backwoods hillbilly movie."

"They would meet up at the local Renaissance fair. It was an opportunity for folks to play dress-up but Clara took her role very seriously. She would go all out, wearing black dress and a pendant draped across her forehead. She would introduce herself as 'the high priestess' and told those who came in contact with her that they would have to 'obey her orders.' This role playing would extend from the Renaissance fair to the online game."

In this fantasy world they created, Schwartz was known as the Priestess of High Chaos. Hulbert became a warrior and Schwartz's protector in the game. The two formed a very close bond.

Lead-up to the Murder

In instant messages and emails police found between Schwartz, Inglis, Pfohl, and Hulbert, Schwartz's fantasy world becomes clear. Schwartz used coded messages, blurring the lines between the game and her real life. In these cryptic messages, she refers to her father as "Old Guy" or "OG" and instead of the word murder uses the code word "tay".

In exchanges between Schwartz and her band of followers, Schwartz described her father as abusive. She claimed that he hit her, pulled her hair, and told her how he disapproved of her friends and her lifestyle. Schwartz even said that she believed her father was trying to poison her. This account is disputed by Schwartz's two siblings, both of whom testified against her during the murder trial and stated that their father had never been abusive.

"Remember she was hanging out with a bunch of self-described rebels," Orange said. "These were kids, young adults, who had problems with authority and didn't fit in. It was really easy for them to believe that older adults had it in for them. Easy for Clara to convince them that her father was all those negative things she said he was."

Before the night of the murder, Hulbert had met Robert Schwartz several times. On one occasion, Clara Schwartz had handed Hulbert a piece of cooked pork that her father had made, claiming it was poisoned. Hulbert tasted it, and in his later written confession to police stated, "I could tell it had been tampered with, both by taste and by smell."

On another visit, Hulbert saw Schwartz's father serving her pork chops and lemon. Hulbert became convinced, with encouragement from Schwartz, that her father was poisoning her food, specifically the pork chops and lemon.

"She was molding his mind," Orange said. "Kyle did not have too much going on upstairs. But he thought of himself as an assassin and that Clara was his queen. He was willing to do anything for her and that made him extremely dangerous."

In the month before the murder, Schwartz and Hulbert's communications became more intense and more directly hinted at the possibility of Hulbert murdering Robert. On November 9, 2001, in an instant message sent to Schwartz, Hulbert asked, "If I was to tay him would you be mad at me?" "Tay" was their secret code word for "kill"—Hulbert was clearly asking Schwartz if he should kill her father.

Schwartz replied, "No. Just don't do it now."

Hulbert continued, asking, "Maybe in a month?"

Schwartz deflected and told Hulbert she didn't want to discuss it online. Instead, she said, "We'll talk about it down here. Take a long walk and talk. I just hate talking about that kind of stuff on here." However, Hulbert's suggestion that he commit the murder in a month must have been well-received by Schwartz, as it was nearly exactly one month later that he killed Robert Schwartz.

The two continued to talk about the possibility of Hulbert killing Schwartz's father through email and instant messages. In another online conversation, Schwartz told Hulbert that if he was to kill her father, "all I ask is that it not traced to me."

Throughout the month of November 2001, Schwartz continued to hint at the possibility of Hulbert killing her father. She told him how her life would be better without her father around and speculated about what it would be like if her father was dead. During this time, Hulbert came to believe that Schwartz's father was going to kill her on an upcoming trip to the Virgin Islands.

At the end of November, Schwartz sent Hulbert $60 via overnight mail. It was later revealed that she intended for Hulbert to use this money to purchase gloves and a do-rag to avoid leaving behind any evidence such as DNA, fingerprints, or strands of hair. With her father's work as an expert in DNA and biotechnology, Schwartz would have been very familiar with the concept of DNA evidence and wanted to be cautious. Schwartz also wanted Hulbert to use the money to buy the gas he would need to drive to her father's house.

The Murder

On the night of December 8, 2001, Kyle Hulbert, Katherine Inglis, and Michael Pfohl got into a car and drove to Robert Schwartz's farm house in Loudon, Virginia. It was a cold, rainy Saturday night. Clara Schwartz was in her dorm room at James Madison University.

"Clara would call her friend Brandy and stay on the phone for over two hours," Orange said. "She would tell of plans her father had of taking her to the Virgin Islands. But what she was really doing was creating an alibi. She was over one-hundred miles away and talking on the phone while her band of followers were killing her father."

Inglis and Pfohl dropped Hulbert off at Robert's house and waited. Hulbert had a 27-inch samurai sword hidden on his person. He knocked on the front door and Robert answered. Hulbert asked if Schwartz was home, and Robert told him she was not. Hulbert asked to come in and get Clara's number.

Robert let Hulbert into his home, a fatal mistake. Hulbert used his bathroom, then followed Robert into the dining room. Here, Hulbert began asking about Robert's alleged abuse of his daughter. He demanded to know if Robert was hurting Schwartz and if he was planning to kill her. Hulbert claimed he told Robert, "I know about your plans. You won't get away with it."

According to Hulbert, Robert had a guilty look in his eyes. To Hulbert, this was proof that Robert was abusing his daughter. Hulbert claimed that Robert smiled at him and smacked him in the face. Hulbert took out the sword and began slashing at Robert.

The attack brought Robert to his knees, where he began pleading and trying to defend himself. Hulbert then stabbed Robert. He claimed that Robert smiled at him, and this infuriated Hulbert. He went into a fit of rage, stabbing Hulbert over and over. According to Hulbert's later written confession, Robert looked up at him and asked "What did I ever do to you?" Hulbert stabbed him one final time after this and killed him.

After the attack, Hulbert rinsed off his sword. He turned off the lights in Robert's home, then left quickly. Hulbert later stated that he heard voices in his head telling him he had to get out fast, because Robert's soul had already left his body.

Aftermath of the Murder

Clara abruptly ended her phone call at 6:30 p.m as she knew that the "assassination" would have been completed. She then waited for heard from Kyle.

Meanwhile, Hulbert went back outside to the car and handed the sword to Pfohl. Pfohl wiped the sword with a towel, wrapped it up, and stashed it in the back of the car. However, the group had encountered a problem. The rain had turned the dirt to mud, and their car was stuck.

Inglis claimed that she asked Hulbert to go back inside and borrow Robert Schwartz's phone to call a tow truck. According to her testimony, Hulbert told her and Pfohl that nobody was home, but she suspected Hulbert had killed Robert. Instead, the group used a neighbor's phone to call for a tow truck. Later, this allowed police to easily identify Schwartz's co-conspirators.

"This really shows how stupid these kids really were," Orange said. "They had just committed a murder and showed up at the neighbor's house to use a phone. Idiotic. Clara herself probably had no idea how stupid the people she had manipulated into doing her dirty work actually were."

The murder of Robert Schwartz wasn't discovered until the following Monday when Schwartz didn't show up to work. Police went to his home and found the scene of the bloody murder. They immediately began investigating Robert's family and looking at Clara Schwartz.

Police pulled phone records from Schwartz's dorm room and found that she had received a phone call right after the murder. Schwartz tried to lie, saying she did not receive any phone calls. When police showed the evidence of the call, Schwartz began blaming Hulbert, saying it was his idea to kill her father.

"Clara played it cool throughout her interrogation," Orange said. "Until she made one slip up. She asked one of the detectives if her sister could phase her out of her father's will. The detective deferred, stating that wasn't his area of concern. But he recognized her intent."

On December 11, Inglis, Pfohl, and Hulbert were arrested and questioned. Inglis was the first to agree to speak to the police. She minimized her own role in the crime. According to her version of events, she and Pfohl dropped Hulbert off with no direct knowledge of his plans. Inglis claimed that Hulbert told them he was going to do a job or a favor for Schwartz. She also claimed that it wasn't until

Hulbert returned with the bloody sword that she suspected he had killed Robert, though she still wasn't certain and didn't act on this suspicion.

"Kyle was still in his own dream world," Orange said. "He thought he was protecting a damsel in distress, his queen. He admitted to the crime although he didn't see himself as a murderer of someone innocent."

The Trial

Inglis' confession brought the entire conspiracy to light. She made a plea bargain with police, and in the end served only a year in jail for her part in the murder of Robert Schwartz. Pfohl confessed as well, pleading to second degree murder. His family made statements asking for lenience, saying the Pfohl was suicidal and easily swayed by Schwartz, wanting to fit in with her group. Pfohl was sentenced to eighteen years in prison.

Hulbert gave a written statement to police, confessing to his crime, but he was not scheduled to have his own trial until after Schwartz.

Clara Schwartz was the only one of the group who ended up going trial. Even before the trial began, Schwartz's own family was against her. Nearly all of her relatives, including her brother and sister, signed a letter asking the judge to keep Schwartz in jail prior to and during the trial. They agreed that she was a danger to herself and others.

The trial took place in October of 2002, less than a year after the murder. Her attorneys argued that she had no real connection to the murder. Instead, they said, this was the result of a misunderstanding between Schwartz and Hulbert. They argued that Schwartz had believed their conversations about murdering her father were all part of their roleplaying game. There was no way, they said, that she could have known Hulbert was going to act on their plot in the real world.

The prosecution had a star witness, however. Schwartz's former boyfriend, Patrick House, came to testify against her. House told how Schwartz had tried to convince him to murder her father before, using the same manipulative techniques based on her roleplaying game. In addition to House's testimony, Schwartz's friend and co-conspirator Inglis testified against her. Inglis described how Schwartz had talked about her father's abuse, provoking Hulbert to commit the murder.

Members of Schwartz's own family testified against her. They argued that she was never abused by her father, painting a picture of a troubled young woman who simply never got along with her father and was interested in the money she might inherit if he died.

On October 15, 2002, after a short one week trial and four hours of deliberation by the jury, Schwartz was found guilty. The jury recommended a sentence of 48 years.

Schwartz's attorneys tried to fight this long sentence recommendation. They argued that the jury had not taken long enough to consider the evidence in full. They also attempted to make the case again during sentencing hearings in February that Schwartz had been abused by her father.

Schwartz's defense team claimed that the prosecution had withheld evidence proving that Schwartz was abused.

During this time, the testimony of one of Schwartz's old high school teachers came to light as well. The teacher stated that Schwartz's father had verbally abused her. Schwartz's family admitted that Schwartz and her father often got into intense arguments, but that there was no abuse in the home.

Finally, the defense attempted to argue that Schwartz suffered from hyperthyroidism, a condition that they claimed inhibited her ability to think clearly and logically. One of Schwartz's uncles, the only family member who testified on her behalf during the entire trial, supported this theory. He backed up the defense's claim that Schwartz was a troubled girl whose mind was clouded by hyperthyroidism, causing her not to realize that she was driving Hulbert to murder her father.

The judge dismissed all of these concerns and upheld the original sentence of 48 years in prison.

Hulbert's Confession

Kyle Hulbert had already given a written statement to police confessing to his involvement in the murder of Robert Schwartz. He had no choice but to either admit guilt in court and accept his punishment or to plead insanity.

Despite a lengthy history of mental illness, Hulbert and his attorneys chose not to pursue an insanity plea. Due to the fact that Hulbert had clearly planned out the crime, an insanity plea was unlikely to work—clearly, he was sane enough to plot a murder.

At a hearing on March 10, 2003, Hulbert confessed to the crime in court. He said he believed it was the right thing to do and would spare the Schwartz family from the agony of another trial connected to the case. Hulbert admitted to feeling guilty, saying he wished he had never met Schwartz and that she had manipulated him into murdering her father.

A psychiatrist testified that Hulbert had many imaginary friends and was seeking a sense of belonging. The psychiatrist claimed that Schwartz gave Hulbert that sense of family and thus manipulated him into doing her bidding.

In the end, Hulbert was given a life sentence for the murder of Robert Schwartz. Ten years were added to the sentence for conspiracy charges as well, ensuring that Hulbert will remain in prison for his entire life.

Although all testimony and evidence pointed to Clara Schwartz as the mastermind behind her father's murder, all those involved suffered the consequences of their actions. Schwartz's ability to manipulate her peers, especially those who already felt rejected by society, was the real deadly force in this case. Without her loyal followers, Schwartz never could have committed the horrific murder of her father.

A DEADLY INTERNET LOVE TRIANGLE

MICHELLE BLUE

Chapter 1

Sharee Miller was a gorgeous, single mother-of-three when she met her husband Bruce Miller. At the time, she was in her early twenties, broke, and weeks away from being homeless.

The couple initially met when Sharee began working at Bruce's automobile scrap yard as a bookkeeper. After only three months, Sharee moved herself and her three kids into Bruce's house and they quickly became a family. Bruce gave Sharee a sense of stability she had never experienced and Sharee was kind, caring, and loving to Bruce.

After only a few more months, the couple married. Domestic bliss loomed on the horizon.

But six months later, Bruce was dead.

Initially, the events that led to Bruce's death were a complete mystery to police until a former homicide detective miles away shot himself in the head and left behind a briefcase of evidence.

How these two deaths were connected would shock police, and lead to one of the most infamous crimes in America.

Chapter 2

Sharee Miller, then Sharee Kitley, was born on October 13, 1971, in Flint, Michigan.

At the time, Flint was a powerhouse of economic growth largely due to the GM Buick and Chevrolet factories that operated in the city. General Motor's history was largely intertwined with Flint—the company's founder had formed the GM company in Flint in 1908. The GM factories in Flint were also the setting of the and iconic 1936-37 Sit-Down Strike—the strike that led to the creation of the United Auto Worker's union.

Flint made money because Flint made cars.

However, the Kitley family did not drink from the city's pool of wealth. They lived on the town's outskirts, a rough working-class neighborhood. They're home was a single-wide trailer smack-dab in the center of a tornado's playground. Sharee was an only child, she was the sole receiver of her parent's attention, but this attention was not desired by Sharee. Sharee's parents fought often, and when they were finished fighting with each other, they'd fight with Sharee.

In mid 80's, when Sharee was in her early teens, GM Motors closed its factories' doors in Flint. The city quickly fell to pieces, ramshackle remains of the auto empire it had once been. The city fell into a deep depression.

As she watched her hometown descend into ruins, Sharee decided to leave her toxic home for good. At the age of 16, Sharee moved in with her boyfriend at the time, and when that ended she couched surfed and work a variety of dead-end jobs, most of which only lasted a few months.

When she was 18, Sharee found herself pregnant and married to an abusive husband. The two shared a home in yet another low-income project in another rough neighborhood left in the dust of Flint's ruined automobile empire. Sharee watched her childhood repeat itself in front of her own eyes, but this time, it was her first-born son who held the starring role of the helpless child. Sharee ended the marriage after she caught her spouse physically abusing the young boy. It was one of the only lines Sharee drew in the sand—you did not harm her children.

Although Sharee took this brave step towards saving her son, history often repeated itself throughout her life. Two more failed attempts at finding a soulmate yielded two more children for the young woman. The single mother-of-three now resorted to frequently moving from low-income house to low-income house and took any odd job she could find—anything to keep her kids off the street.

Chapter 3

In 1997, Sharee was a single mother-of-three who was three breaths and an electricity bill away from being homeless. During an attempt to keep her kids safe and housed, Sharee took a job as a bookkeeper with B&D Auto, a small auto scrapyard that fit right in in the middle of Flint's automobile history.

Sharee had been hired despite having little-to-no experience keeping books in the past. She had convinced the boss, Bruce Miller, that she was hard-working, a fast learner, and desperate for a paycheque. And that seemed to be enough. That and the fact that Sharee was a stunner. Her bright blonde hair only drew more attention to her enrapturing icy blue eyes.

Bruce was a kind and generous soul. He took a chance on Sharee and it seemed to pay off. Only a few months after Sharee had begun working at the scrapyard, she and Bruce moved their relationship from the office to the bedroom. It wasn't long before Sharee and her three kids moved in with Bruce. The four now lived in a stable, secure home for the first time in any of their lives.

Bruce and Sharee married only months after they first met. Bruce, who has twenty-one his new bride's senior, thought he had finally found the perfect wife. Young, sexy, and loving. It was all he had ever wanted.

Her new life with Bruce was also a dream come true for Sharee. She had finally found a man that treated her right, and in him, she also found security. Ten years ago, she had left her own unhappy parents and embarked on a life of poverty and abuse. Now, she was sitting in the living room of a big house, watching her children—the true loves of her life—swimming in Bruce's above-ground pool. It was the idyllic life she never thought she could have.

But idyllicism did not suit Sharee.

Chapter 4

While Sharee lived the life she had always wanted for herself and her kids, Bruce's own family began to have doubts behind Sharee's motives.

Initially, Bruce's family took no issue with the fact that Bruce's wife was so young. The couple looked so happy and in love, they formed a perfect family. Bruce was even in the process of adopting Sharee's three boys. But things slowly began to change.

Sharee began to take advantage of her new wealth. She no longer worked at the scrapyard but began selling Mary Kay Cosmetics to other bored housewives instead. She began spending every penny of her earnings, and a whole lot more of Bruce's, on luxuries she had never been presented with before. She bought expensive jewelry and clothes, she got her first credit card plus a few more, and she bought an expensive computer for the home.

Bruce, however, did not partake in his family's worries. He was as happy as ever the day Jerry Cassaday stepped into his office and shot him square in the chest. Bruce understood Sharee's desire to buy things, he enjoyed watching her be careless with money for the first time in her life. And most of all, Bruce was proud that she began selling cosmetics door-to-door. An entrepreneur himself, he found Sharee's new profession to be ambitious. Bold. He had no qualms when Sharee brought home expensive dress after expensive dress, and he was nothing but proud when she showed him the computer she claimed was to help her keep track of all her sales.

If you had asked Bruce, he would have said the couple was as happy as could be.

Sharee, evidently, was not happy. Although she was pleased with the security her marriage to Bruce brought, she was bored. She was living the life of a housewife and simply got restless. She started going online and frequenting chat rooms where she could talk to strangers and meet new men. She could talk to these new men and Bruce would be none the wiser.

It was the perfect situation for Sharee. She got to keep the stable home life she knew she needed while engaging in the excitement of meeting new singles and falling in love without the latter threatening the first. In short, she got to have her cake and eat it too.

But this quickly fell apart. Soon, the satisfaction Sharee got from speaking to these men online began to fade. She needed more. She wanted to meet these men, feel their touch. This yearning was fresh in her mind the day she met Jerry Cassaday.

Chapter 5

Jerry Cassaday was working as a pit boss in a Reno casino. Before that, he had been a homicide detective and police officer for the Marshall Police Department and the Cass County Sheriff's Department. He began frequenting online chat rooms after his wife left him. He was lonely and had always wanted a family. He went online hoping to find companionship and an honest connection with a beautiful woman. Instead, he found Sharee Miller.

The two hit it off immediately. For Cassaday, it was love at first sight. He was enraptured by the blue-eyed blonde-haired twenty-something-year-old. There was only one problem: Sharee lived in Flint, Michigan and Cassaday was stuck in Reno, Nevada. They had no way to meet without arousing the suspicions of Sharee's husband Bruce until the perfect opportunity arose—a Mary Kay Cosmetics conference was announced. The location? None other than Reno, Nevada.

Sharee jumped at this opportunity to meet Cassaday in person and the spark they had struck up online burst into flames when they met in person. The two spent every free minute they had together, and Sharee even accompanied Cassaday to work. She would sit at his table and play hands of blackjack. When Cassaday finished for the night, the two would go back to Sharee's hotel room.

While Sharee was honest about being married at the time, she altered many details about her life in Flint to her favor. It was all part of the fantasy she had built up for herself online. Sharee told Cassaday that her husband was a high-ranking member of the mafia who frequently beat her and mistreated her children. They weren't in love, she was just too afraid to leave. Cassaday, who was in his mid 30's at the time, had always wanted a family and was aghast when Sharee told him the details about how her current husband treated herself and her kids. Little did he know it was all a lie.

The picture Sharee painted of her husband Bruce was so far away from the handsome, family-orientated business man that he really was. She wasn't describing reality, she was describing a fantasy. And Cassaday had bought it.

After Sharee inevitably left her new lover behind to return home to Flint, Sharee kept up their flame by sending numerous naked photos by email to Cassaday. They kept in constant touch through emails and instant messages. The two kept in touch so frequently that members of Bruce's family could later recall him complaining about the amount of time Sharee began to spend on her new computer. He knew something was up, he just wasn't sure what.

Sharee continued to build on the fantasy she had created with Cassaday. As well as nude photos, she would send him photos of herself covered in bruise-coloured makeup claiming they were from Bruce. On one special occasion, she went old school and snail-mailed Cassaday a tape labeled For Jerry's Eyes Only...

As Sharee fell deeper into the rabbit hole she had dug, two things became clear to her: the first, Cassaday was completely and utterly under her control, the second, she liked her new fantasy more than her real marriage.

Chapter 6

Sharee Miller's life had taken such a turn from her younger years. She had a stable life, a happy home, and a loving husband. But somehow, this was no longer enough for Sharee. Addicted to the danger of the unknown, Sharee had become bored in her easy marriage. She craved more.

She found the perfect path out of her marriage in Jerry Cassaday. Initially, the thrill of an affair was enough for her, but this eventually grew old—especially when her affair became online only.

Usually, when someone grows tired of their online relationship, they break up with their partner and cease communications. This was not the case with Sharee and Jerry Cassaday. When Sharee grew tired of her online affair with Cassaday she did not stop communications—she increased them. Although she had fallen out of love with the ex-homicide detective, she still needed him for one very specific purpose. He was going to kill her husband for her.

Cassaday had fallen madly in love with Sharee. He believed she was married to an abusive husband who has a high-ranking mafia player. He feared for his beautiful girlfriend and would do almost anything to protect her. Almost wasn't good enough for Sharee though. Sharee was going to use Cassaday to get out of her marriage, and to do so, she was going to have to make him mad first. Mad enough to kill.

Sharee's plan seemed foolproof. Bruce, her husband, was alone at his auto scrapyard a lot, and he always carried a large amount of cash on him, roughly $2000, in order to make change for his customers. Sharee saw this as the perfect opportunity. Someone could easily kill Bruce at his work with no witnesses, and better yet, if they took the cash on him, it would look like a robbery-gone-wrong. This would inevitably point police away from herself. All she needed was someone to pull the trigger.

Chapter 7

At some point during their online relationship, Sharee realized that she had Cassaday wrapped around her finger. She had seduced him in online and in-person and had maintained this enrapturement through sending him endless emails and seductive videos. Sharee began to use this power she had over Cassaday to make him angry. She had already painted her kind, gentle husband to be an abusive mafia man, but she needed more.

About a month after meeting with Cassaday in person, Sharee went to her local pharmacy and purchased a pregnancy test. She knew she wasn't pregnant—she had had her tubes tied after the birth of her third son—but she needed Cassaday to think she was. She went home, took photos of herself with her stomach pushed out, and sent them to Cassaday along with photos of the pregnancy test, which she had drawn lines on so it appeared to be a positive test. To make the lie seem more real, she also sent an image of her third child's sonograms.

I'm pregnant, she wrote Cassaday, with your first children. Twins.

A few weeks later, Sharee sent Cassaday more pictures of her stomach. This time, however, she coated her belly in blue and purple makeup first.

He killed our beautiful babies was the message sent along with the photos.

Cassaday was devastated, his lover's abusive husband had just taken from the world what he thought would be his opportunity to have a normal life with the woman he loved. He fell into a severe state of depression. Cassaday could not take the news. He could no longer watch the woman he loved destroyed by her own oppressive husband. No. He was coming to town to free Sharee and finally have the family he'd always wanted.

Sharee was ecstatic. Through one later-debated series of instant messages, Sharee slowly revealed her perfect plan on how Cassaday should murder Bruce. The whole of Sharee's plan was summed up in only a few damning sentences.

I'll call Bruce at 5pm and tell him to call me when he's leaving. Pull up to the left side of the building, right to the door. He'll be at the desk inside. Take his wallet. Take the whole thing.

Chapter 8

On November 8, 1999, Jerry Cassaday drove from Reno to Flint to kill the man he thought killed his twin babies and repeatedly beat the love of his life.

He followed Sharee's instructions to the word. At 5pm he pulled up to Bruce Miller's auto scrapyard, went inside, shot Bruce in the chest, and took Bruce's wallet. Bruce was on the phone with Sharee at the time, just as she had planned. Sharee had chosen to listen to her husband die.

Cassaday's experience as a homicide detective meant that he could commit the crime without leaving forensic evidence behind. He left the scrapyard office without leaving a single finger or footprint and took Bruce's wallet without ripping the pocket, a general characteristic of a rushed robbery. Investigators were also unable to recover any trace fibers or hairs from the scene or Bruce's body.

After committing the crime he had spent the majority of his life solving, Cassaday turned his car around and headed straight back to Nevada.

Chapter 9

A few hours after listening to her lover shoot her husband, Sharee called her brother-in-law Chuck Miller. She frantically told him that Bruce was missing, he hadn't come home for dinner and his work phone wasn't working. She convinced Chuck to drive out to the scrapyard to check on his brother.

When Chuck arrived, he was affronted with a horrible scene—Bruce was laying face down on the ground dead from a gunshot wound to his chest. His telephone receiver was on the ground next to his face. Within an hour, a full team of homicide investigators were on the scene.

Due to the lack of physical evidence at the scene, investigator's initially had little to go on. The main motive appeared to be robbery, just another day in Flint.

Sharee was brought in for questioning but was never suspected by police. She had been at home all day with her children and several friends. They simply wanted to ask her if she had any idea of who would want her husband dead, and Sharee was prepared for this.

Sharee told detectives that one of her former boyfriends John Hutchinson had owed Bruce several thousands of dollars. Bruce and

Hutchinson had several arguments about this as well as the tumultuous state of Sharee and Hutchinson's former relationship.

Hutchison unluckily had no solid alibi. He quickly emerged as the key suspect in Bruce's murder.

To make things worse for Hutchinson, he had agreed to take a lie-detector test to prove his innocence, but the examination did not go smoothly. In the middle of the test Hutchinson collapsed and ended up going to the hospital. Not only had he failed the few questions he had been asked, but he was so clearly stressed about the test that he had physical symptoms.

The general feeling amongst investigators was that Hutchinson had killed Bruce, they just couldn't prove it. While his autopsy revealed that Bruce had been shot by a 20 gauge shotgun, Hutchinson did not own this type of gun and investigators failed to find one during a search of his home.

Eventually, much to Sharee's delight, the case went cold. It wasn't until a seemingly unrelated suicide miles away took place before police had any reason to suspect Sharee.

Chapter 10

After he returned to his home in Reno, Jerry Cassaday expected his relationship with Sharee Miller to continue as usual. He believed that they would continue to date long-distance until the murder investigation cooled down. Then, Sharee would begin a new life in Reno with Cassaday.

This, however, was not the case.

Sharee barely contacted Cassaday after the death of her husband. She didn't initiate any conversations and stopped replying to his emails altogether. Cassaday, still deep in the world of lies Sharee had created, began to panic.

A few weeks after killing her husband, Cassaday decided to pay Sharee a visit to make sure she was doing okay. When he arrived at her home in Flint, his world fell apart.

Sharee was at home with her three kids and a new boyfriend.

She had double-crossed Cassaday within weeks of the murder. Cassaday instantly returned to the state of depression he had been in when he believed that Bruce had killed his baby twins-to-be.

Sharee and Cassaday never spoke again, and Sharee had almost entirely forgot about her ex-lover when police started knocking on her door again.

Chapter 11

Seven hundred miles away from Sharee and Flint, in Kansas City, Missouri, Jerry Cassaday was found dead in his home, a gun in his hand, Bible in his lap, shot in the head. Cassaday could not live with the crimes he had committed for love, especially knowing that the love he felt wasn't real. It was too much for him.

Before he killed himself, Cassaday took measures to ensure his death would be connected back to Sharee and Bruce Miller's murder. Next to his body, police found his open briefcase which contained his suicide note addressed to his parents and a printed transcript of extensive instant messaging conversations. Outside in the trash, investigators also found a scandalous video of a young woman dancing naked addressed directly to Jerry.

Police showed clips of this video to Jerry's neighbors in order to identify the woman dancing. Several neighbors were able to identify Jerry's online girlfriend Sharee, who lived in Flint. When Kansas City police called the Flint sheriff's office to get more information about Sharee, Flint police were astounded. They instantly knew they had been duped by the blonde, beautiful widow.

When she was identified by Kansas City police, Sharee was immediately connected not only to Cassaday's suicide but also back to her ex-husband Bruce's murder. In his suicide note, Cassaday revealed that he had been the one to kill Bruce. Sadly, it was evident that he still believed many of the lies Sharee had told him. He stated in his note that he had to do it, Bruce had killed his children and that was something he couldn't let go. Even if it meant destroying his own life in the process.

He also described Sharee's role in the murder plot. He stated that she had encouraged him to commit the murder and helped him plan it. He could not have done it without her help. And he had provided investigators with the transcripts to prove it.

Sharee miller was brought in for questioning where she claimed she did not even know Jerry Cassaday. She stuck to this story until police revealed that they had the tape of her dancing, addressed in her handwriting as being For Jerry's Eyes Only. After this, she was forced to change her story. It was undisputable evidence that they had had a relationship.

Sharee then told police she had met Jerry in a computer chatroom while just messing around, trying to figure out something new to do. Computer forensic experts then confiscated both Sharee and Cassaday's computers. What they found inside answered some important questions but raised many others.

Investigators easily found their way into Sharee and Cassaday's private online conversations. They found incriminating evidence on Jerry's computer—the online copy of the instant messaging conversation in which Cassaday and Sharee discussed Bruce's murder. When they confronted Sharee with these messages, she had a planned response: Cassaday was framing her.

Sharee told investigators that in the triangle of herself, her ex-husband Bruce, and Jerry Cassaday, Cassaday was the scorned lover. After she got bored with her online affair, she tried to cut contact with Cassaday, but he wouldn't let her. She claimed that Cassaday had forged the messages to implicate her in something she had never been apart of. Investigators thought that this claim was far-fetched, so they reached out to AOL, the company that hosted the instant messaging service Cassaday and Sharee used to communicate. Surprisingly, AOL took Sharee's side on the issue—it was possible for the messages to have been forged.

Investigators were now tasked with proving the legitimacy of the instant messages that showed Sharee had helped plan Bruce's murder with Cassaday. Under court order, AOL released information about Sharee and Jerry's computer activity. They confirmed that both Jerry and Sharee had been online and logged into the AOL service the same day at the same time for the same length of time as the instant message indicated. Police also found handwritten notes copied in Sharee's writing that listed information found in the messages. If they had been forged, Sharee would not have known this information in order to write it down.

Sharee was now trapped. Although she continued to maintain her innocence, investigators continued to find more and more damning evidence against Sharee.

Sharee had taken steps to cover her online footprints. A day and a half after the death of her husband she had called AOL to change her first name, last name, and her address. After she learned of the suicide of Jerry Cassaday, she did the same thing again. She was clearly worried about the content of her online messages being traced back to her.

Once investigators had confirmed the legitimacy of the messages, they were able to read the diary of Sharee's relationship with Cassaday. They were able to see how she was able to bring Cassaday to a boil, both sexually and emotionally. She brought him into her world the way she wanted him to see it.

Sharee had used her body, in so many ways, to intrigue, seduce, and trap the ex-homicide detective. The only thing that brought her down in the end was Cassaday's conscience on his dying day.

Further, Sharee's actions after her husband's death provided a possible motive for Bruce's murder other than Sharee's freedom. Money.

While Sharee had been loose with money during her marriage, she had gone over-the-top after her husband's death. She used Bruce's life insurance money to dramatically renovate her new inherited home within weeks of his death. She bought herself a new car and spent thousands of dollars on a plethora of items.

When Bruce died, Sharee inherited the family home she had grown so attached to as well as large sums of money both from Bruce's life insurance policy and also from the sale of his auto scrapyard business. Most significantly, though, Sharee had inherited her freedom without having to sacrifice her own and her children's secure, stable life.

Chapter 13

In December, 2000, Sharee went on trial for murder and conspiracy to commit murder.

Throughout the trial, Sharee continued to maintain that the instant messages were forged, as she was innocent of everything. She was simply the victim of an angry lover's broken heart.

The prosecutor's relied heavily on forensic science in their case against Sharee Miller—specifically, on the forensic computer analysis which proved the authenticity of Sharee and Cassaday's messages.

Sharee's trial was a short one. It did not take the prosecutors long to form their case, and the defense presented little-to-no evidence to support Sharee's claims that she was being framed by a dead man.

Sharee was found guilty on the charges of second-degree murder and conspiracy to commit first-degree murder. She was sentenced to life without the possibility of parole.

But this was not the end of Sharee's story.

Chapter 14

In 2009, Sharee Miller was released from prison after serving only nine years of a life without parole sentence. Her release was mandated by a U.S. District Judge who believed that the convicted killer had grounds for a new trial. This was because Jerry Cassaday's suicide note had been presented as damning evidence against Sharee in court despite the fact that Cassaday could not be cross-examined regarding the information in the letter.

Sharee spent a whole three years outside of bars. During this time, she kept a fairly low profile. She stayed in Flint with family, who she spent the most time with. She also spent the three years reconnecting with her sons—the children she spent most of her younger life fighting to support. Sharee's luck finally seemed to be turning in her favor.

But lady luck is fickle. In 2012, Sharee was ordered back to prison by the U.S. Supreme Court. The court disapproved of Sharee's release and mandated that the judge repeals her earlier decision to grant Sharee a new trial. The Supreme Court believed that there was enough additional evidence presented by the prosecutors, with no viable defense to counter it, that the outcome of the trial would have been the same had the suicide note not been presented at all.

Sharee's lawyers told the public that she was simply "disappointed" by her return to prison.

After returning to prison, Sharee and her lawyers quickly filed several appeals targeted at both the decision to return Sharee to court and her original guilty conviction, both of which were lost. Sharee was set to spend the rest of her life in prison for good this time.

That again seemed like the end of Sharee's story until late April 2016.

Seventeen years after manipulating Jerry Cassaday into killing her husband, Sharee Miller admitted her involvement in the crime for the first time through a letter addressed to a County Judge.

In this letter, Sharee claimed that she got caught up in the fantasy world she created with Cassaday. She like being the victim. It was more exciting to her than her real, stable life. However, she quickly found herself in too deep. She had created a monster and the only real way she saw of getting out was through the murder.

If Bruce were to die, neither he nor his family would ever have to discover what she was doing behind his back.

Sharee stated in her confessional letter that she did not enjoy watching her husband die. She wrote, "I had sixteen and a half hours to stop it. And I didn't. I knew it was going to happen and I allowed it. I allowed a man to kill another man based on my lies and manipulation."

She also used her letter as an opportunity to publicly recant the horrible image she had painted of her husband through her messages with Cassaday. She confirmed that Bruce was nothing but a wonderful husband. He had never laid a finger on her, and he always treated herself and her three children with the utmost kindness and respect. She regretted being the reason her children lost such a wonderful father figure—something she had always wanted for them.

While Sharee certainly believed that her confession would put an end to the long-standing controversy surrounding her case, the kind of controversy that inspired both a novel and lifetime movie about her crime, it actually perpetuated a new kind strand of controversy.

To many, especially to Bruce's loved ones, Sharee's confession letter seemed too crafted to be sincere. Sharee was the woman who had manipulated men to kill and die for her all through text. Now, she seemed to be trying to manipulate her way to an earlier release through the same medium.

Whether Sharee will claim another victim as a fool, this time a court judge, is yet to be seen.

9 798224 038916